for Bathenkosi Sphesihle Luphalule aka MoMo, Tetris B Mountaingoat

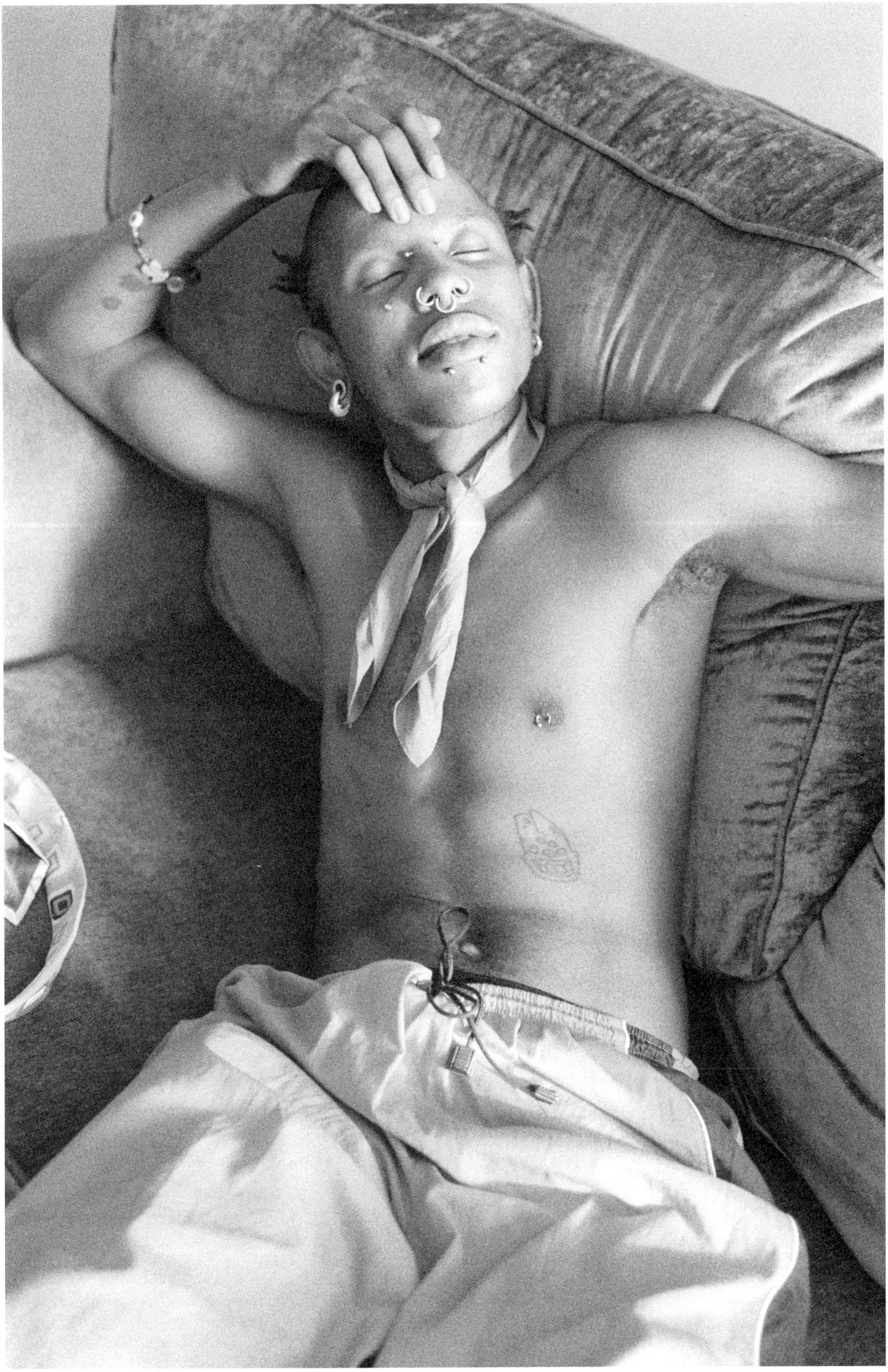

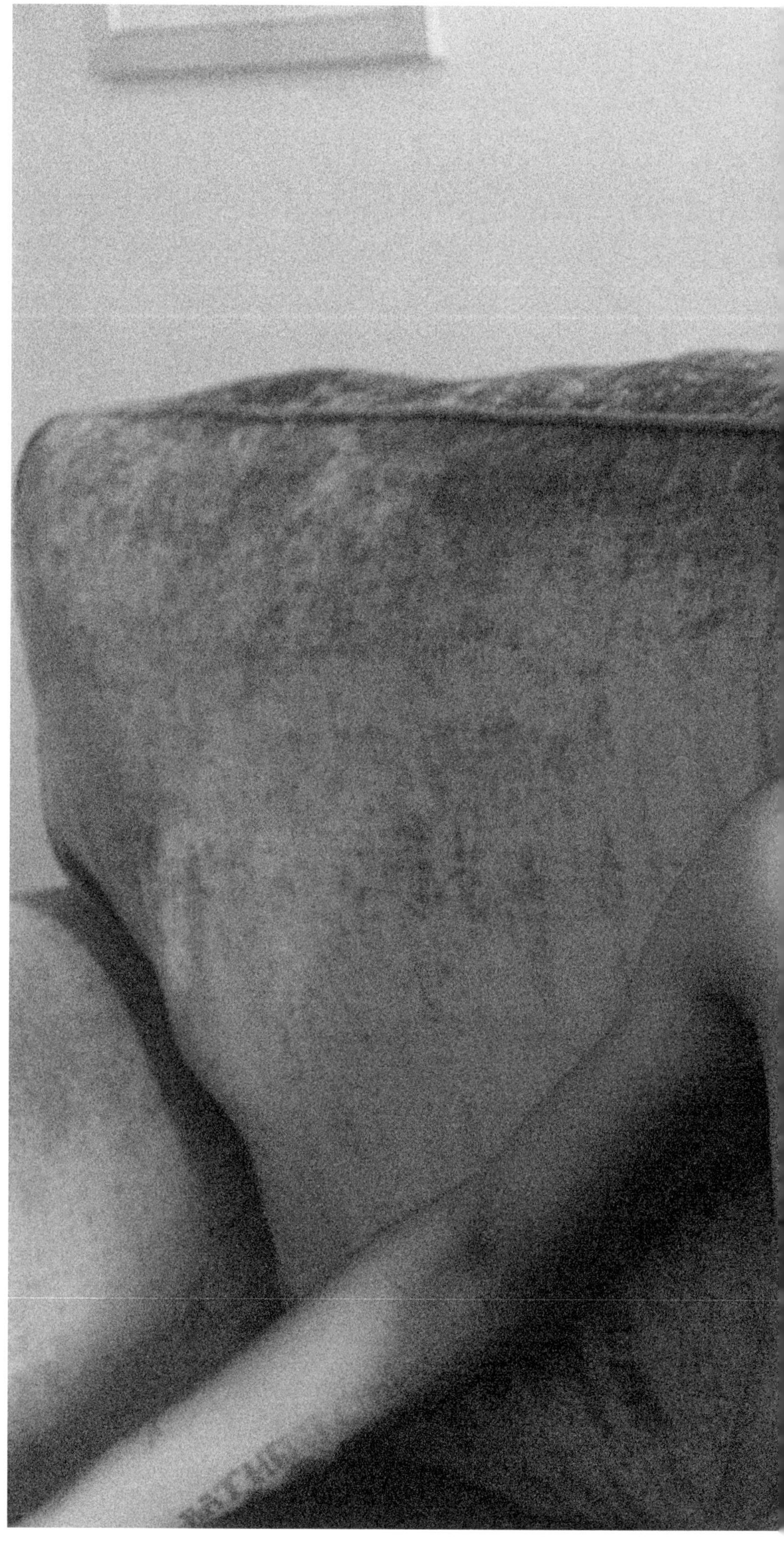

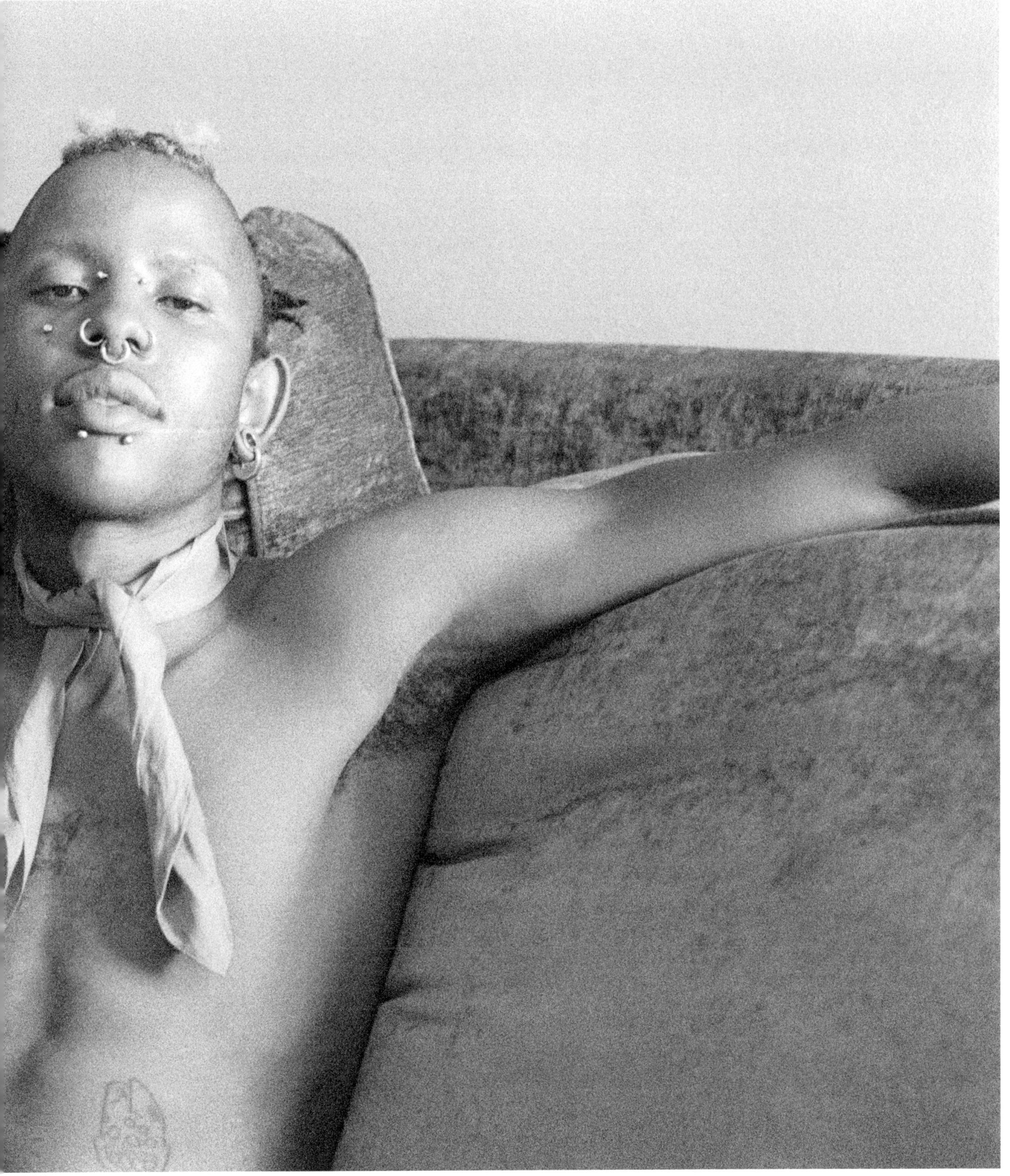

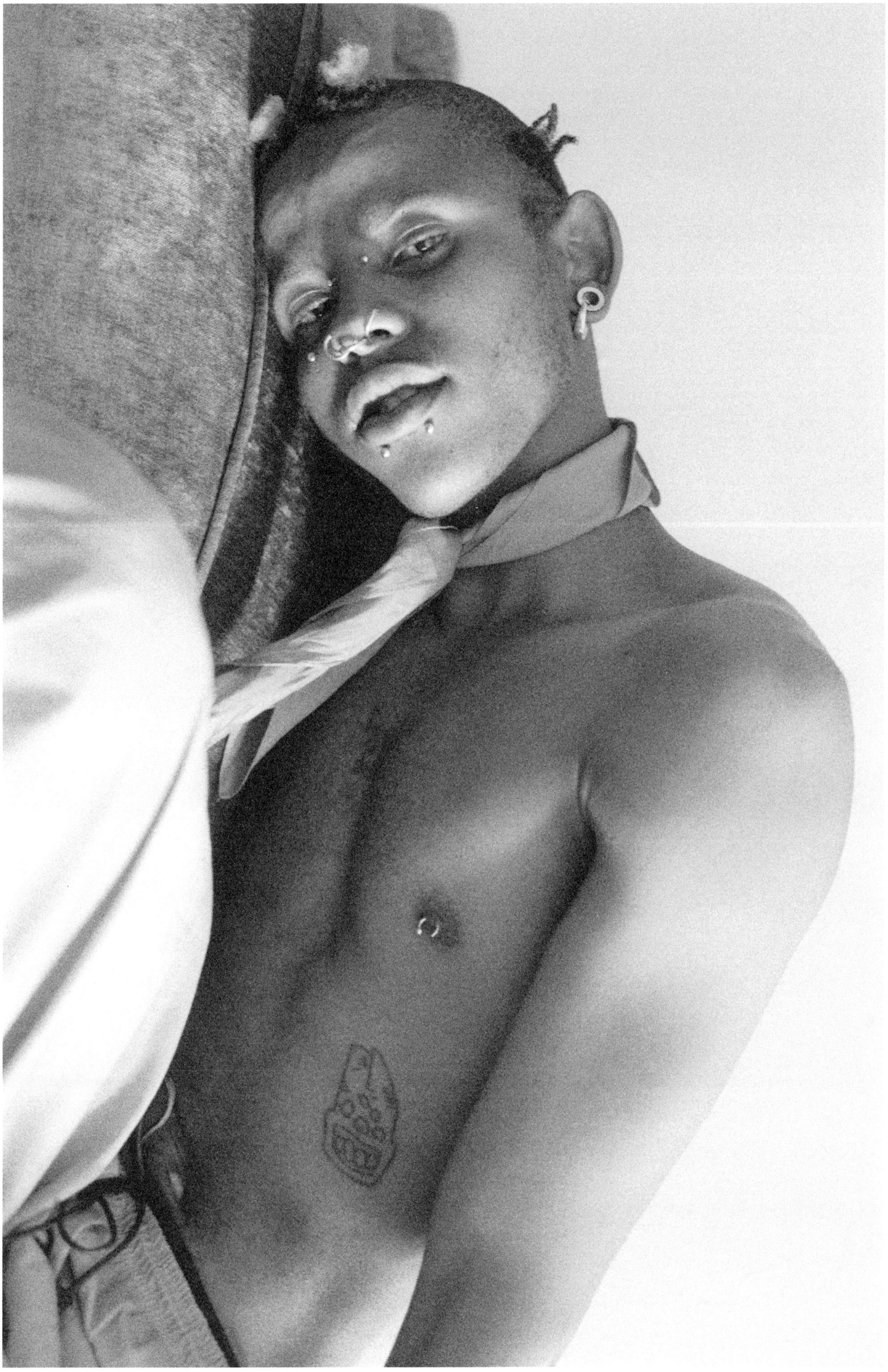

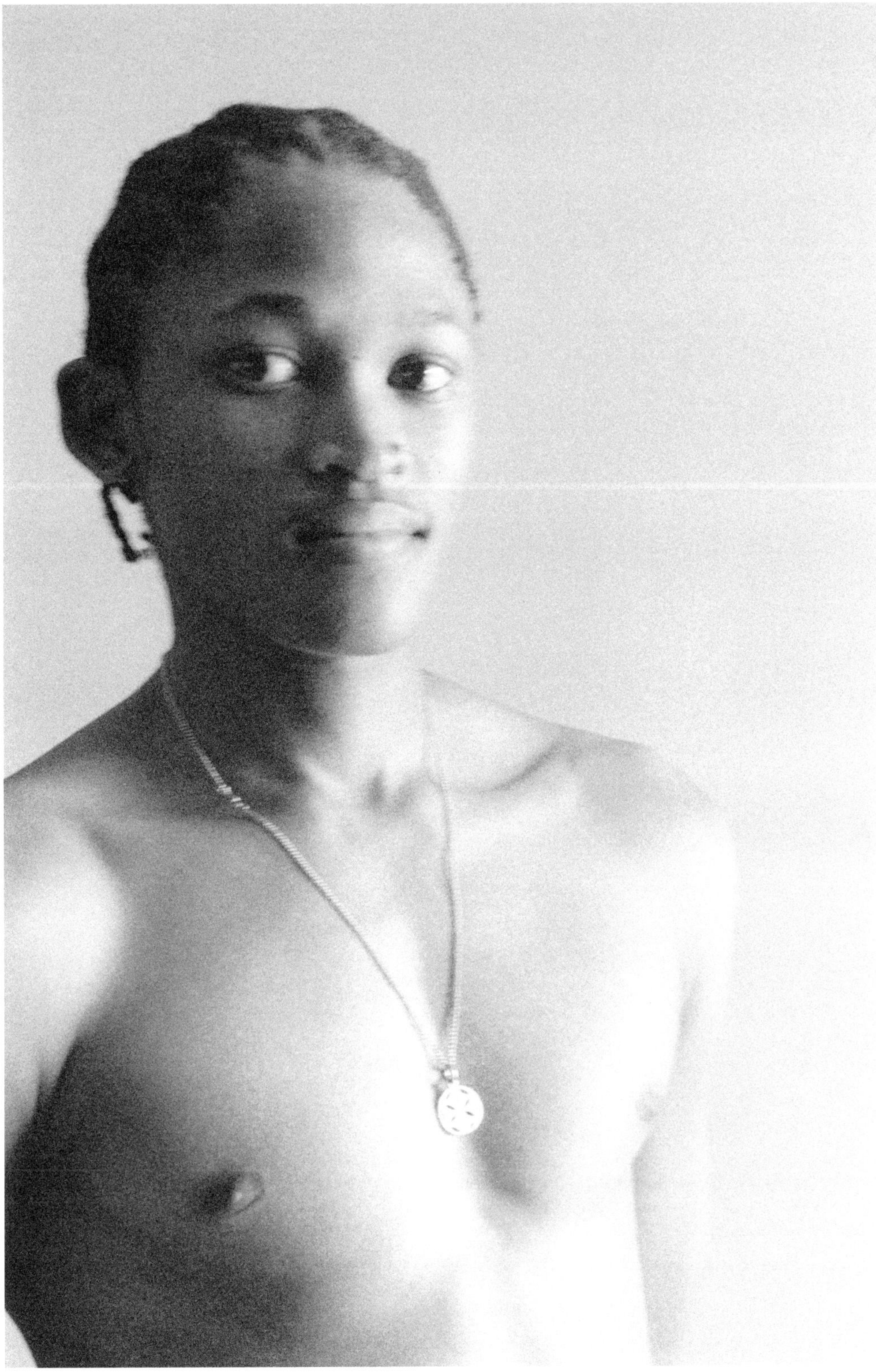

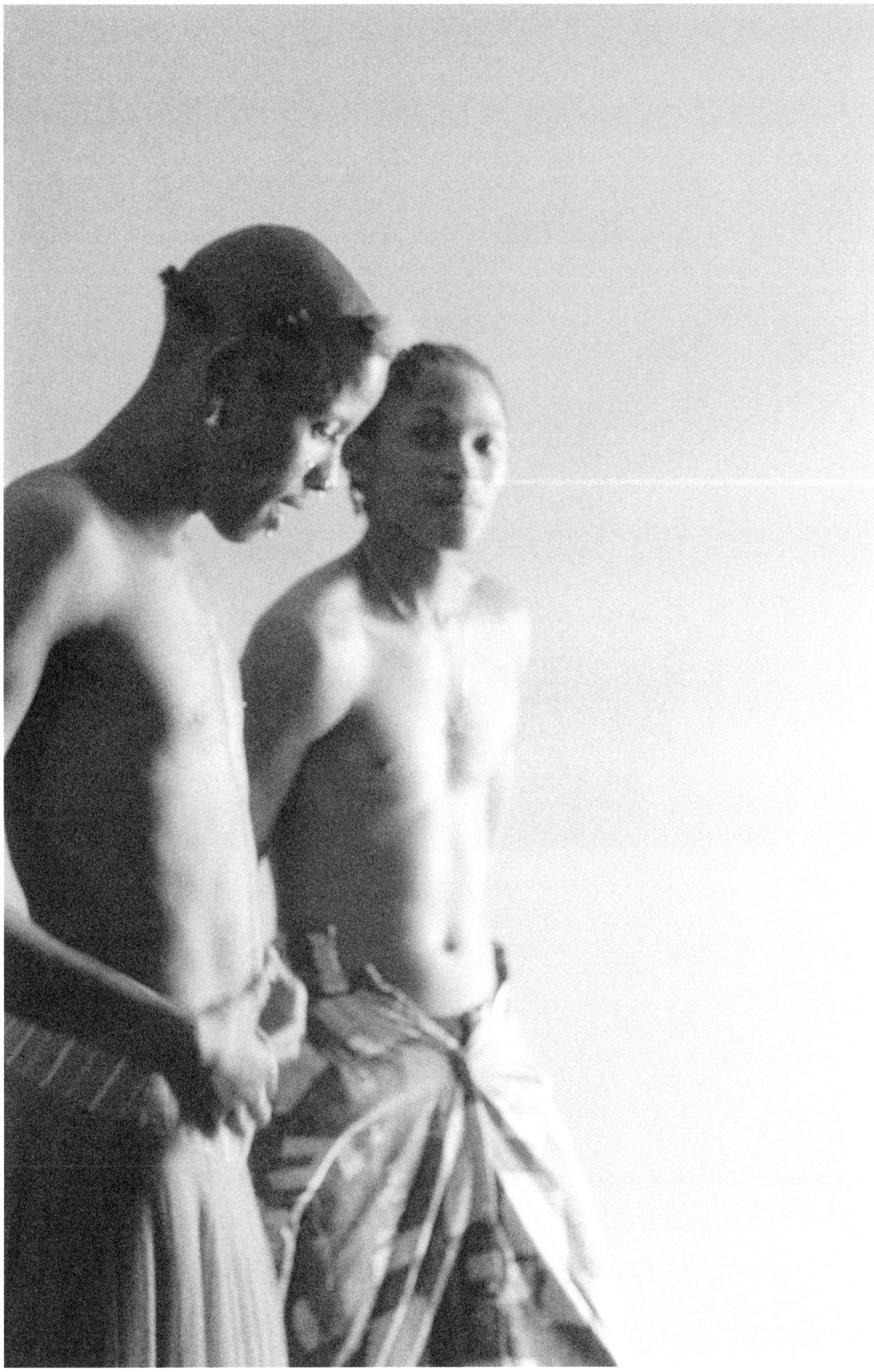

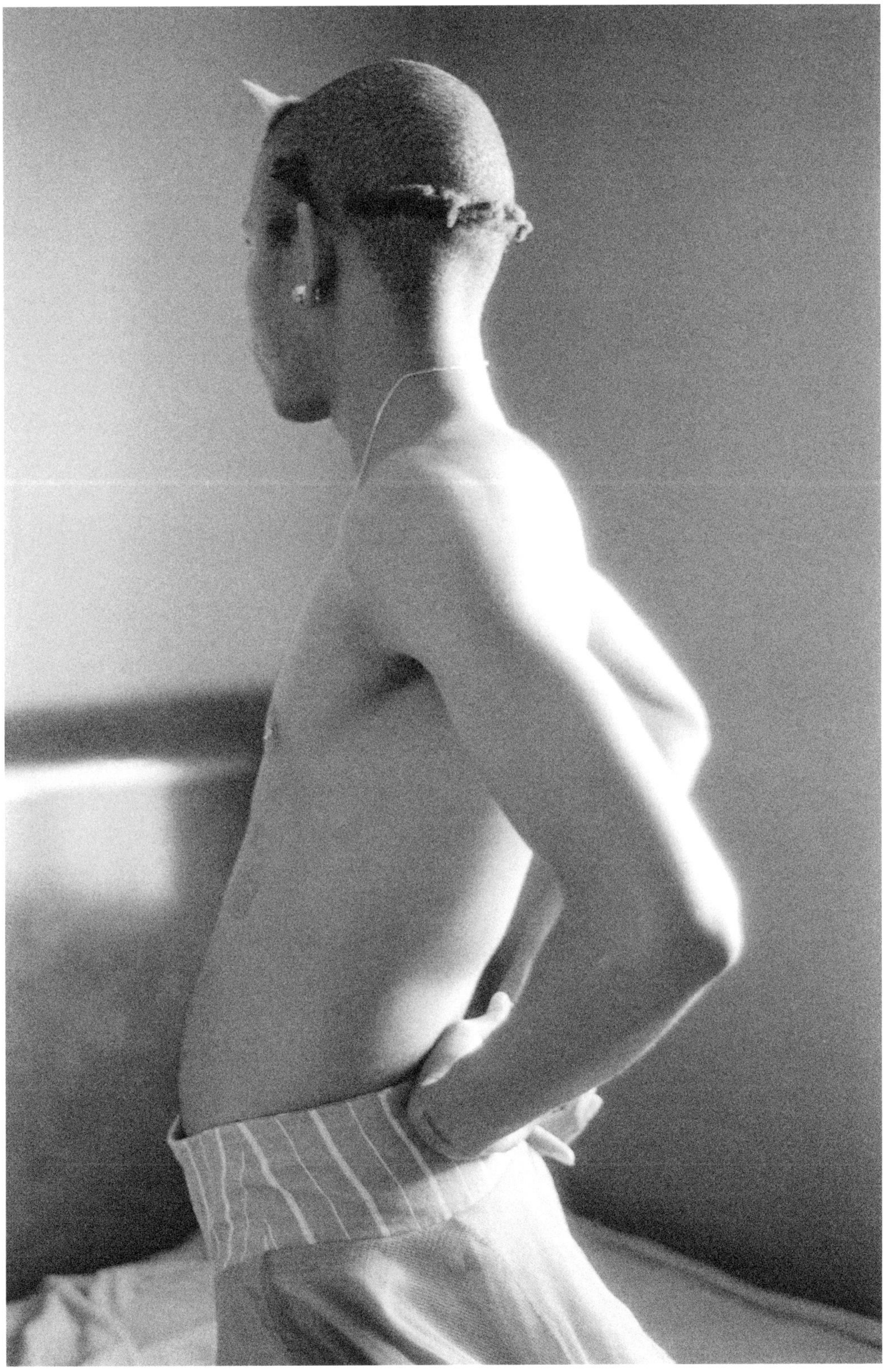

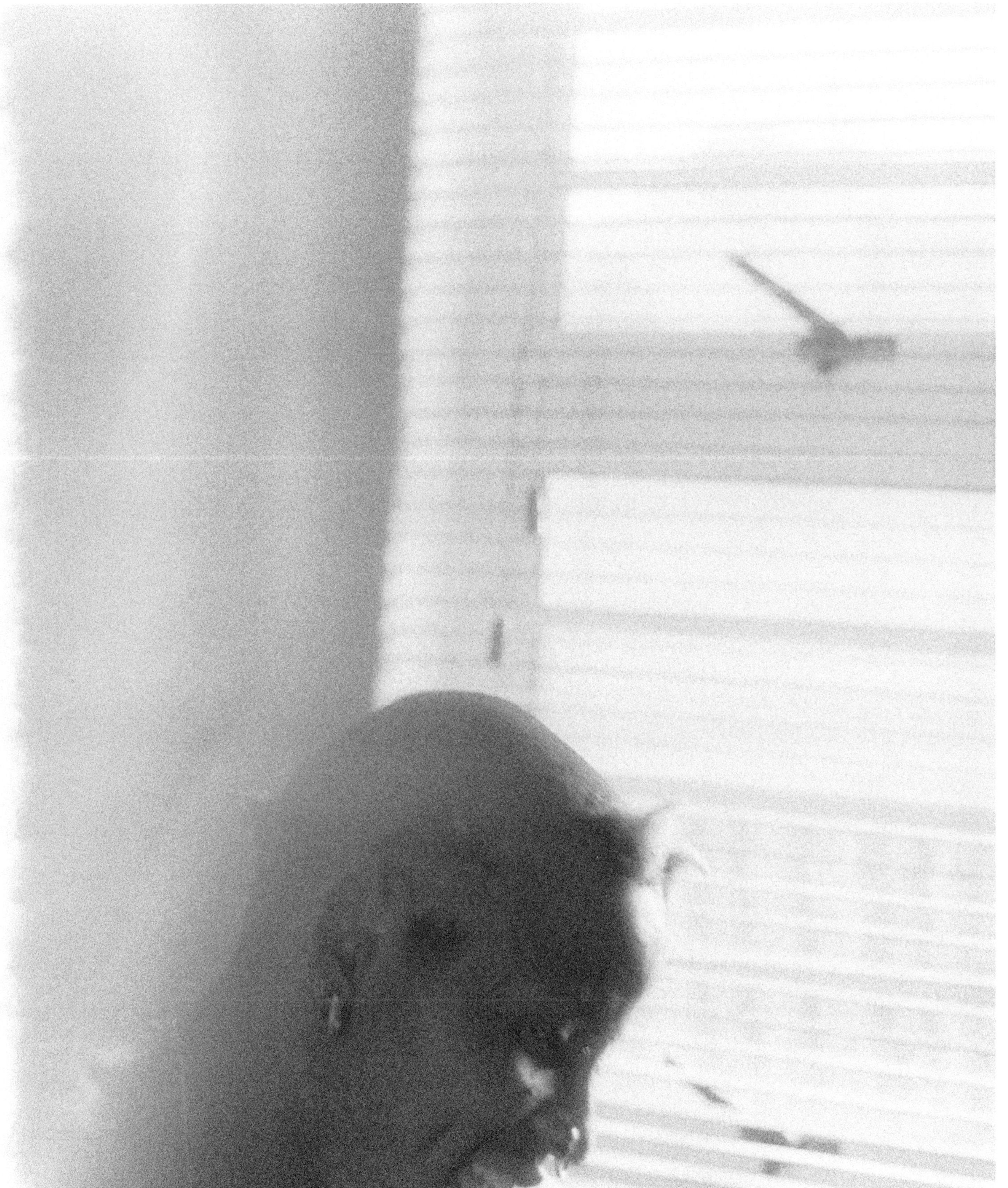

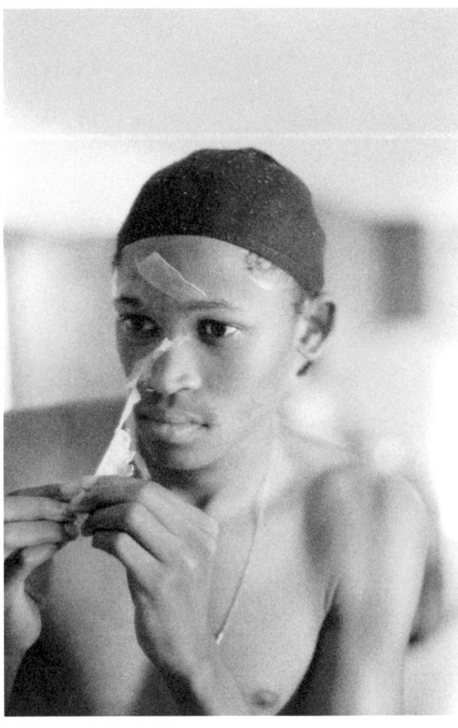
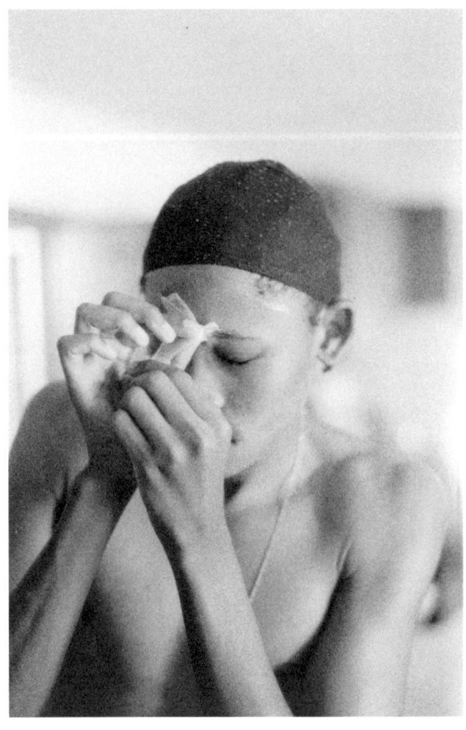

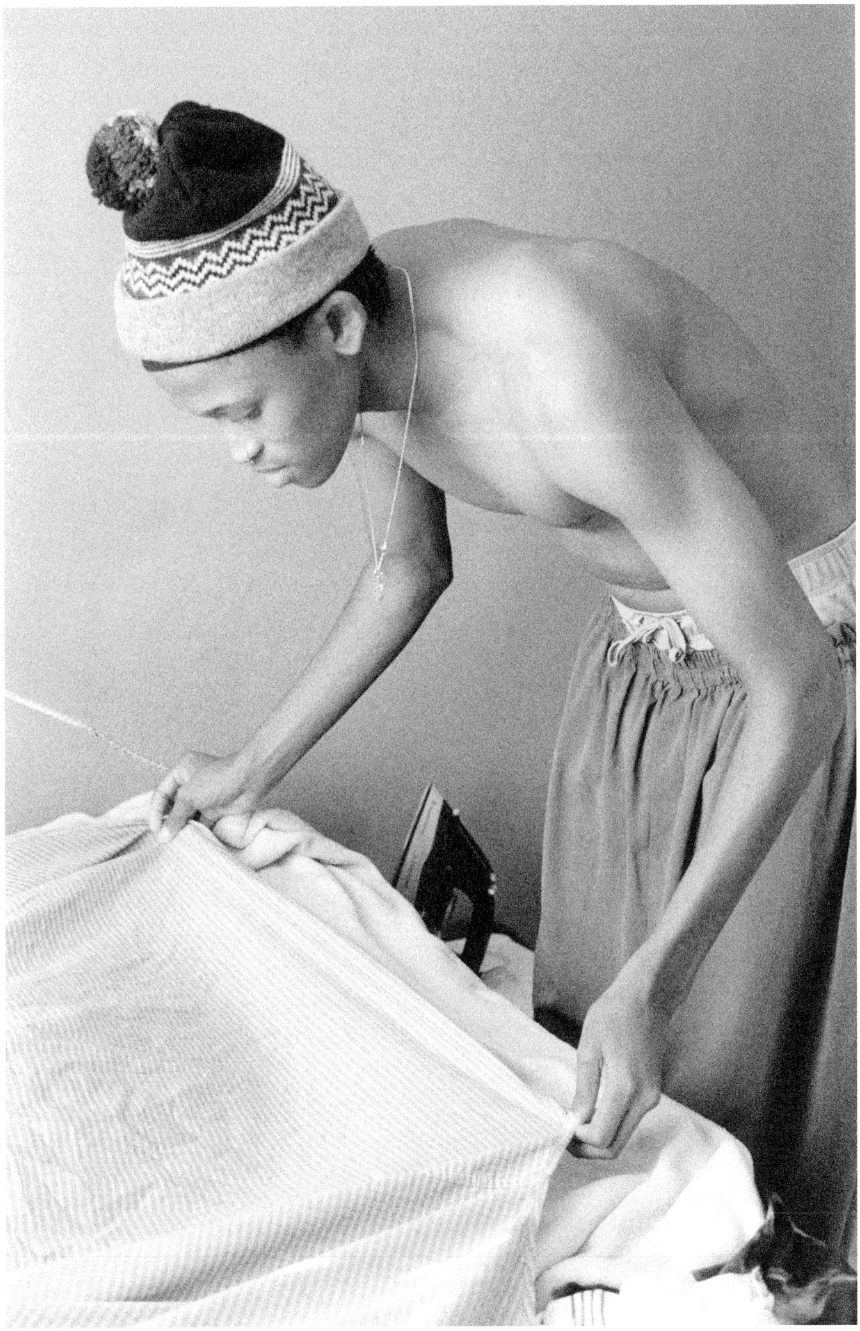

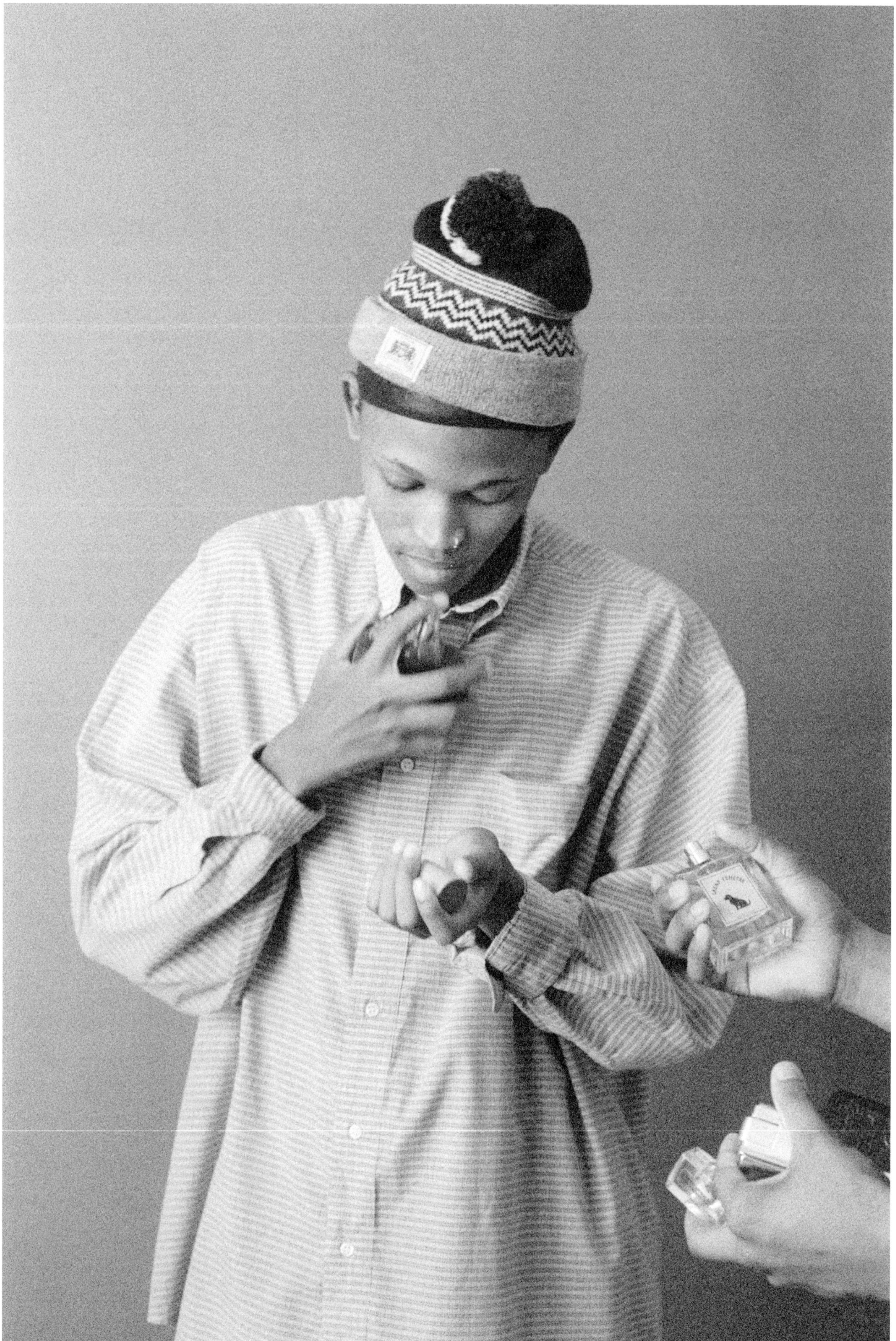

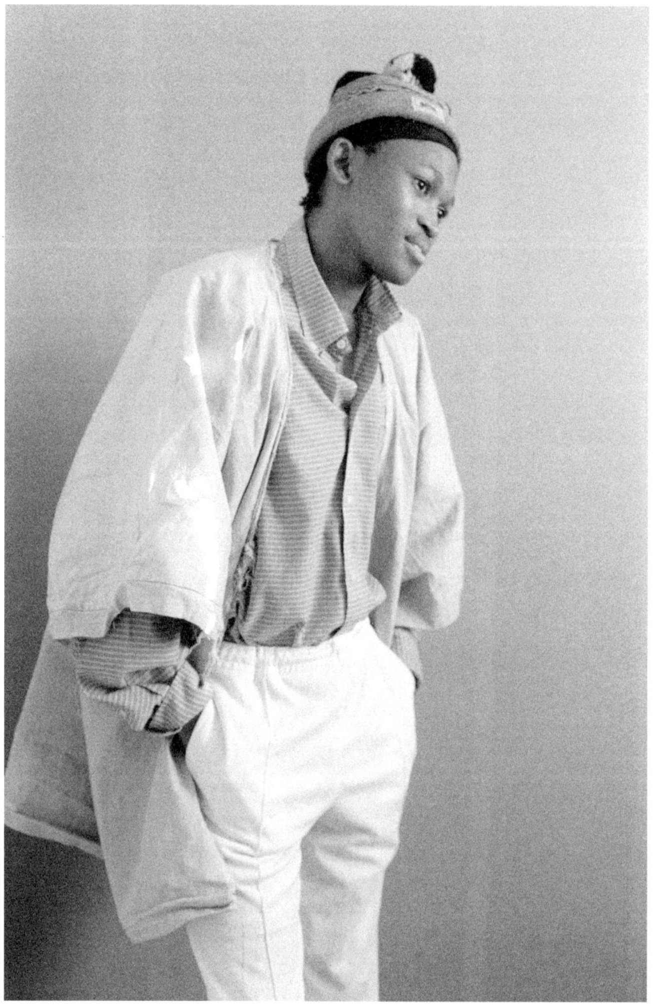

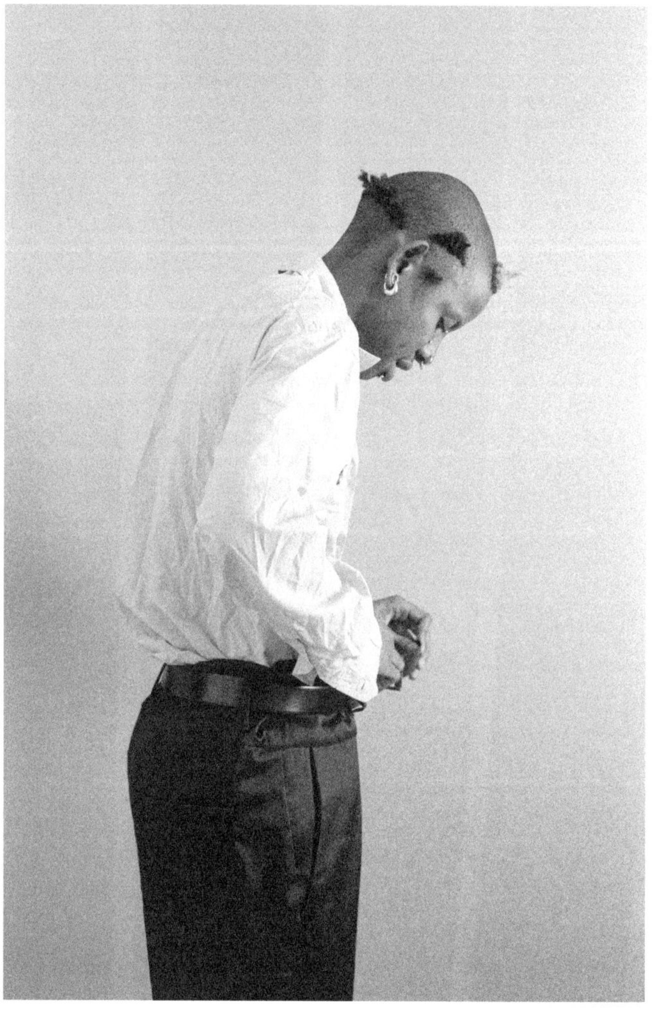

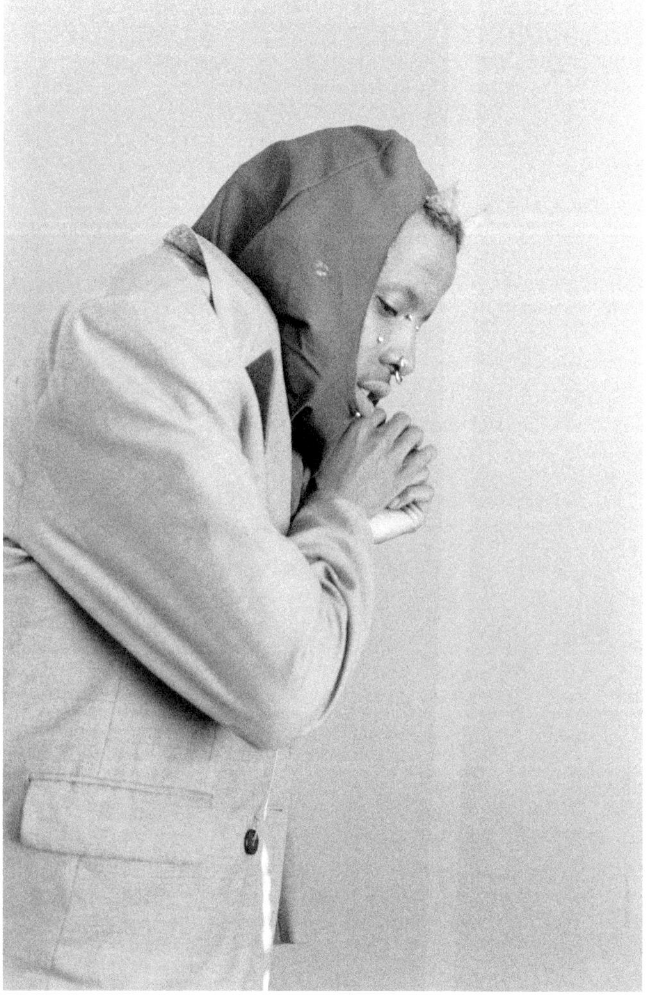

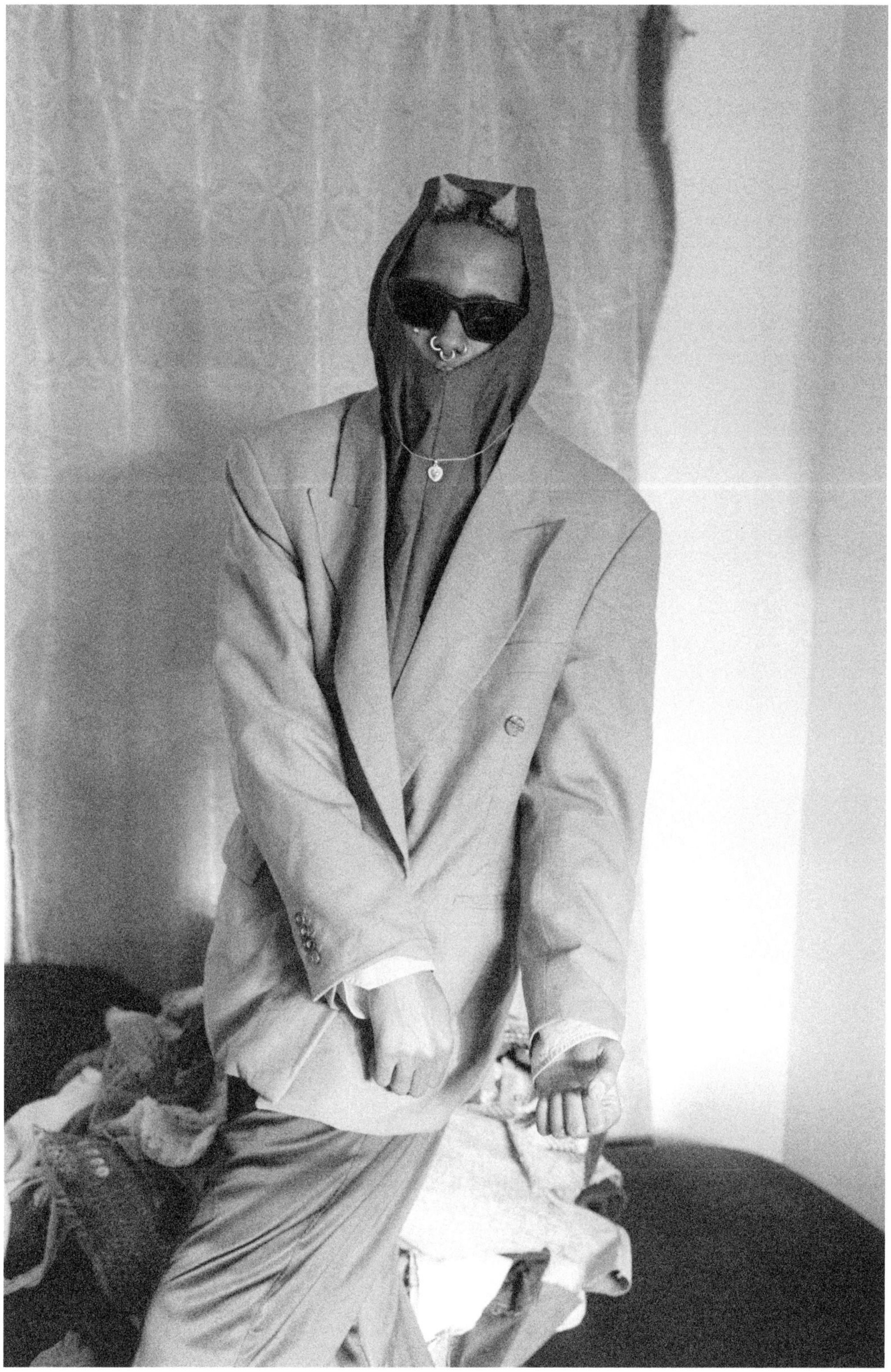

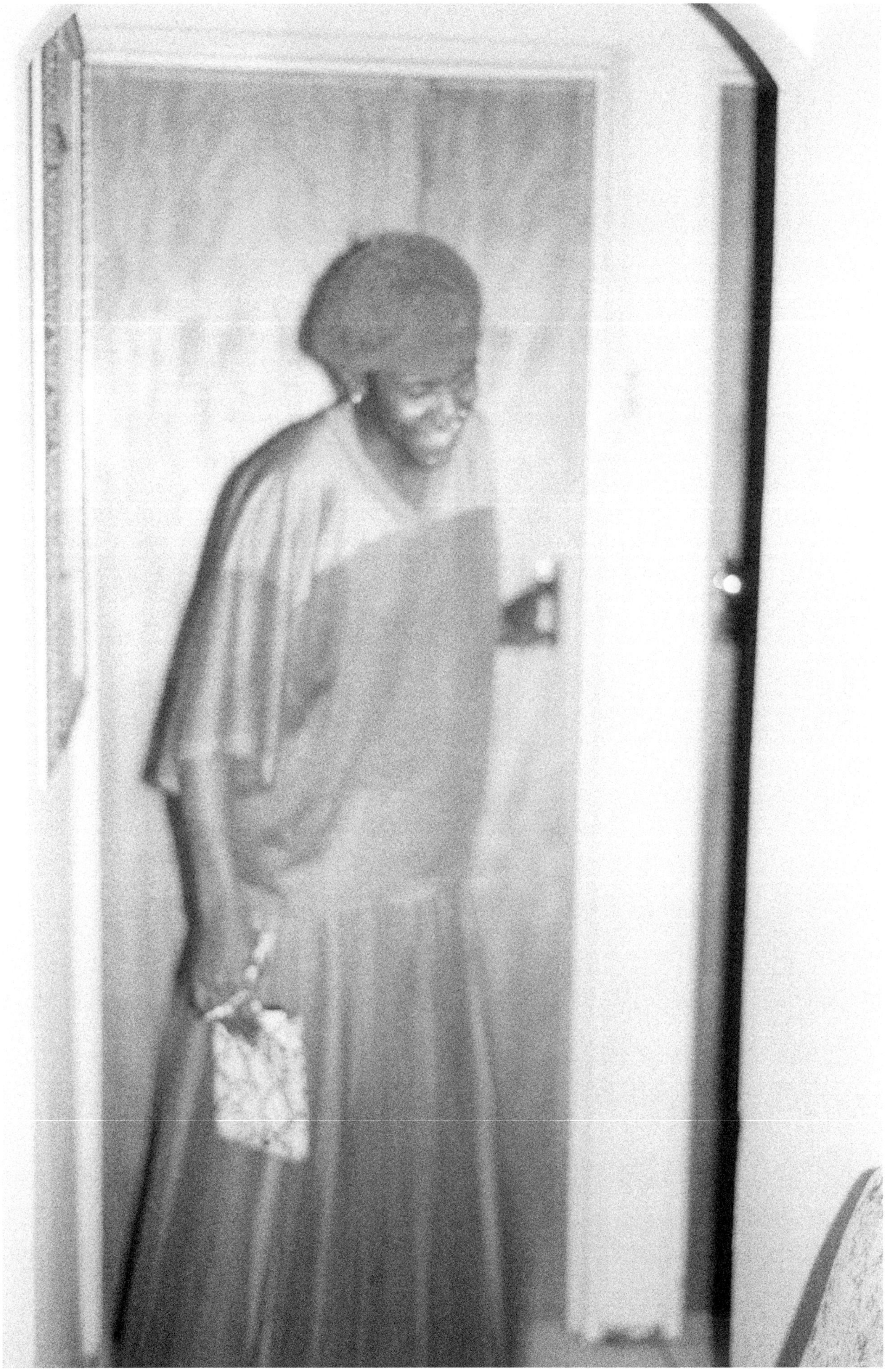

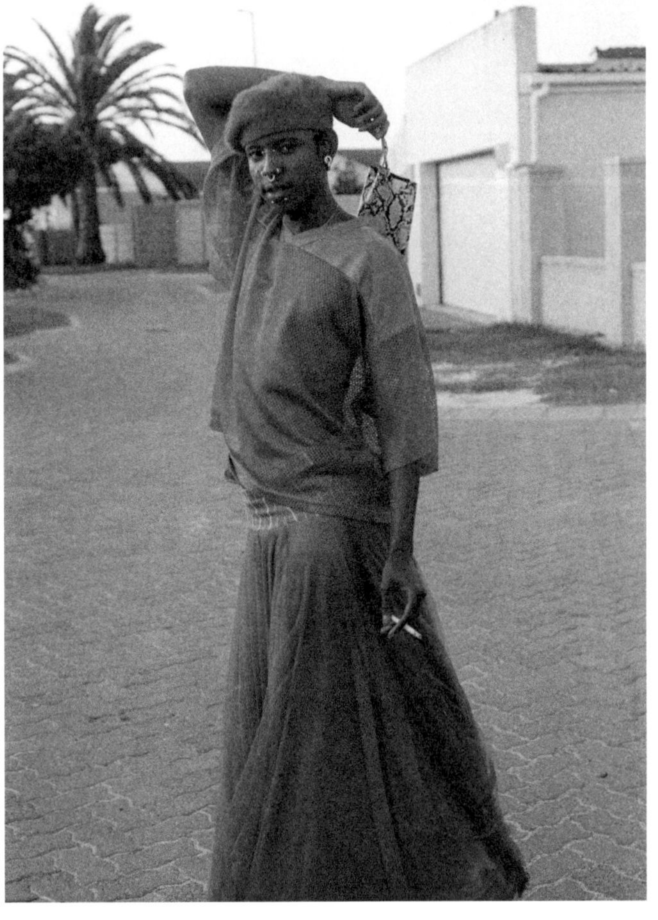

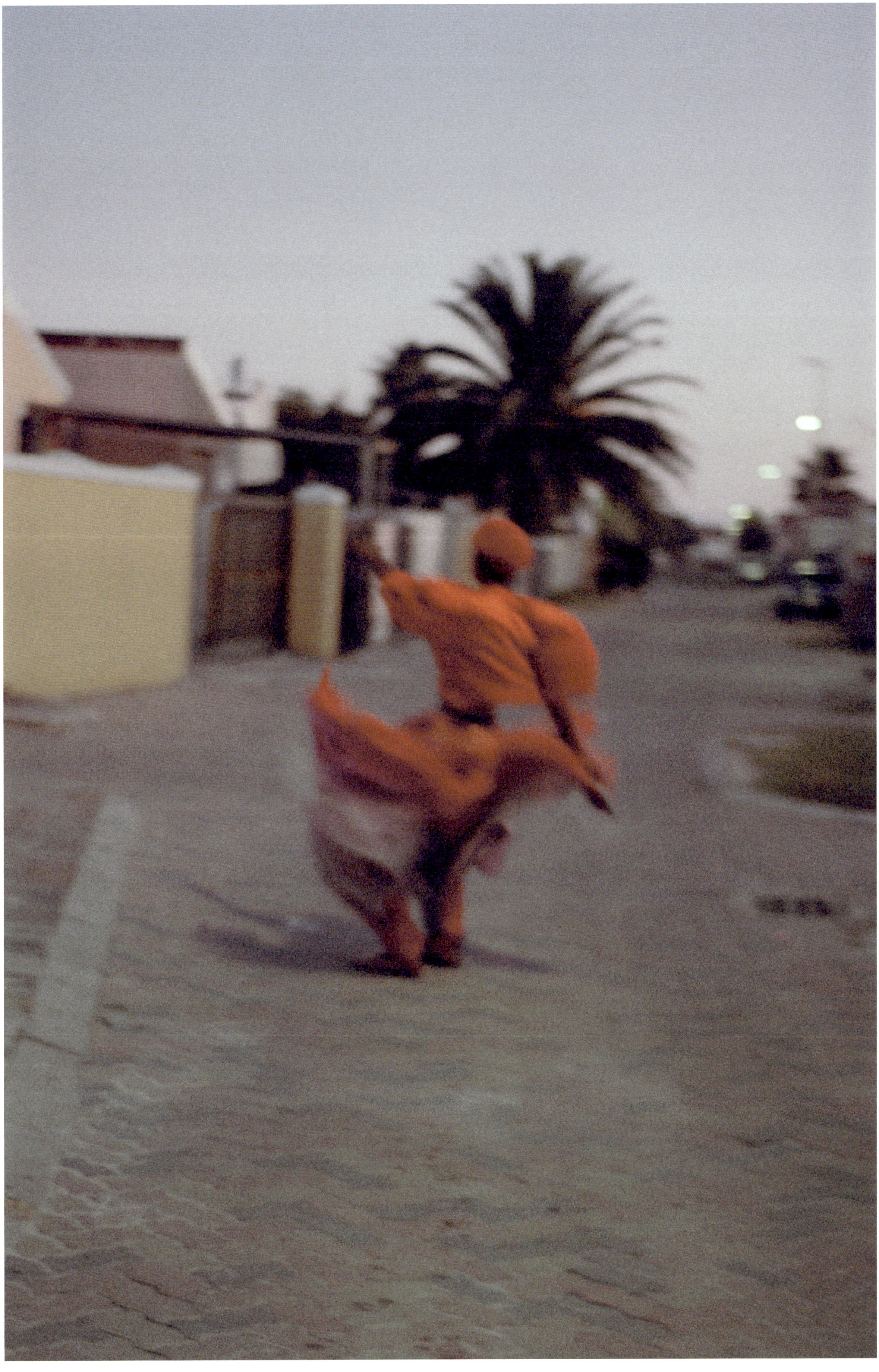

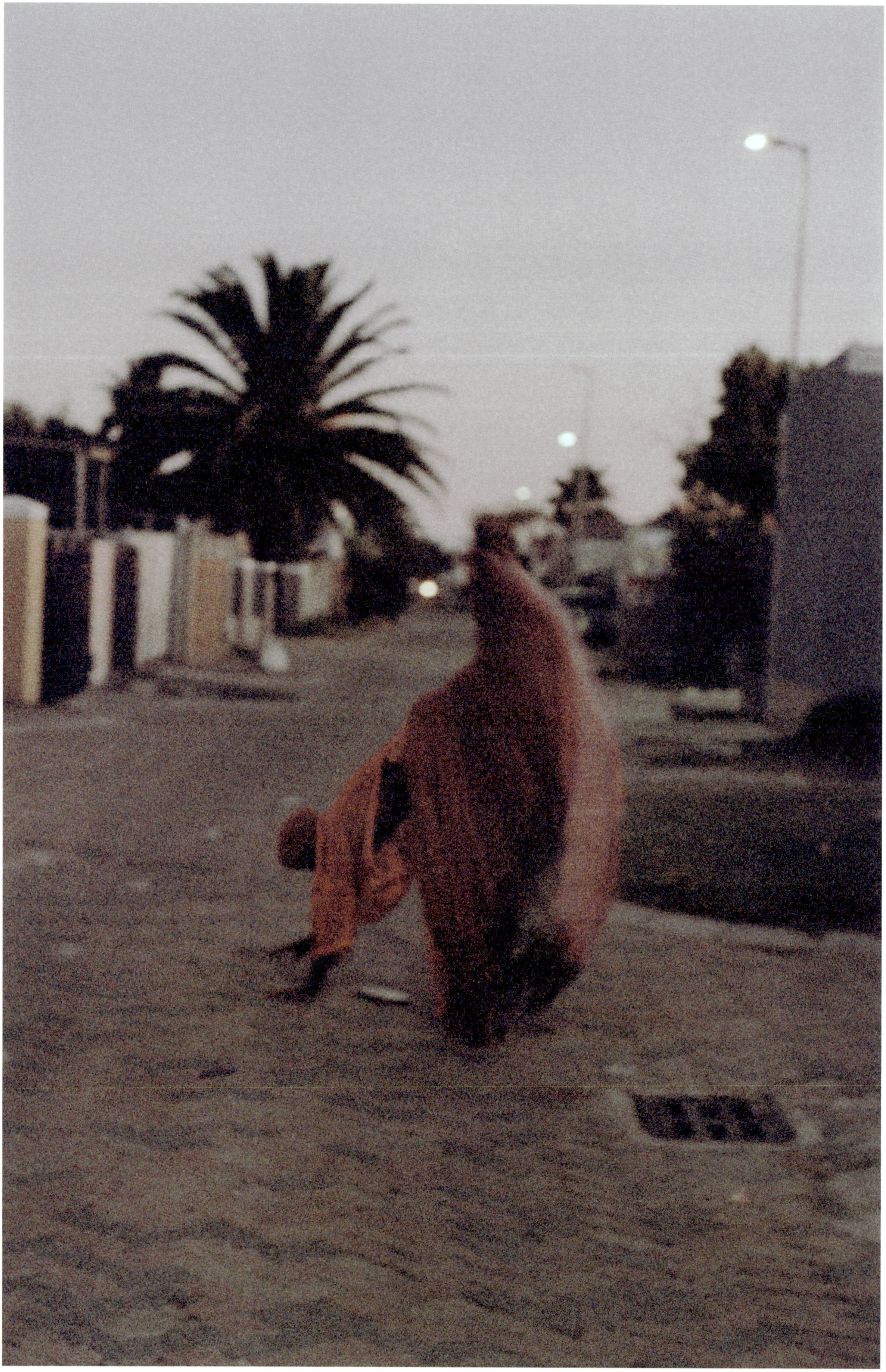

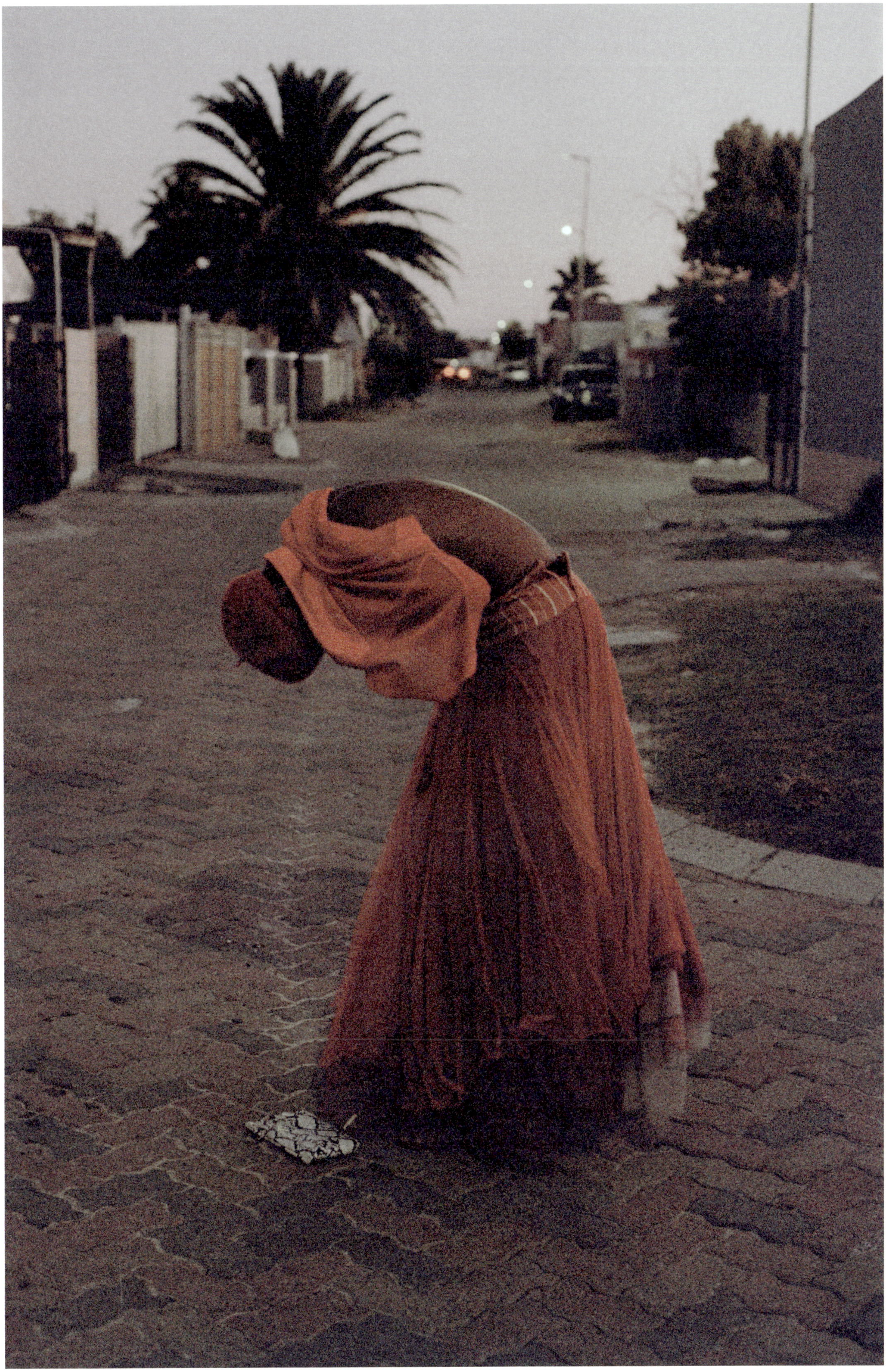

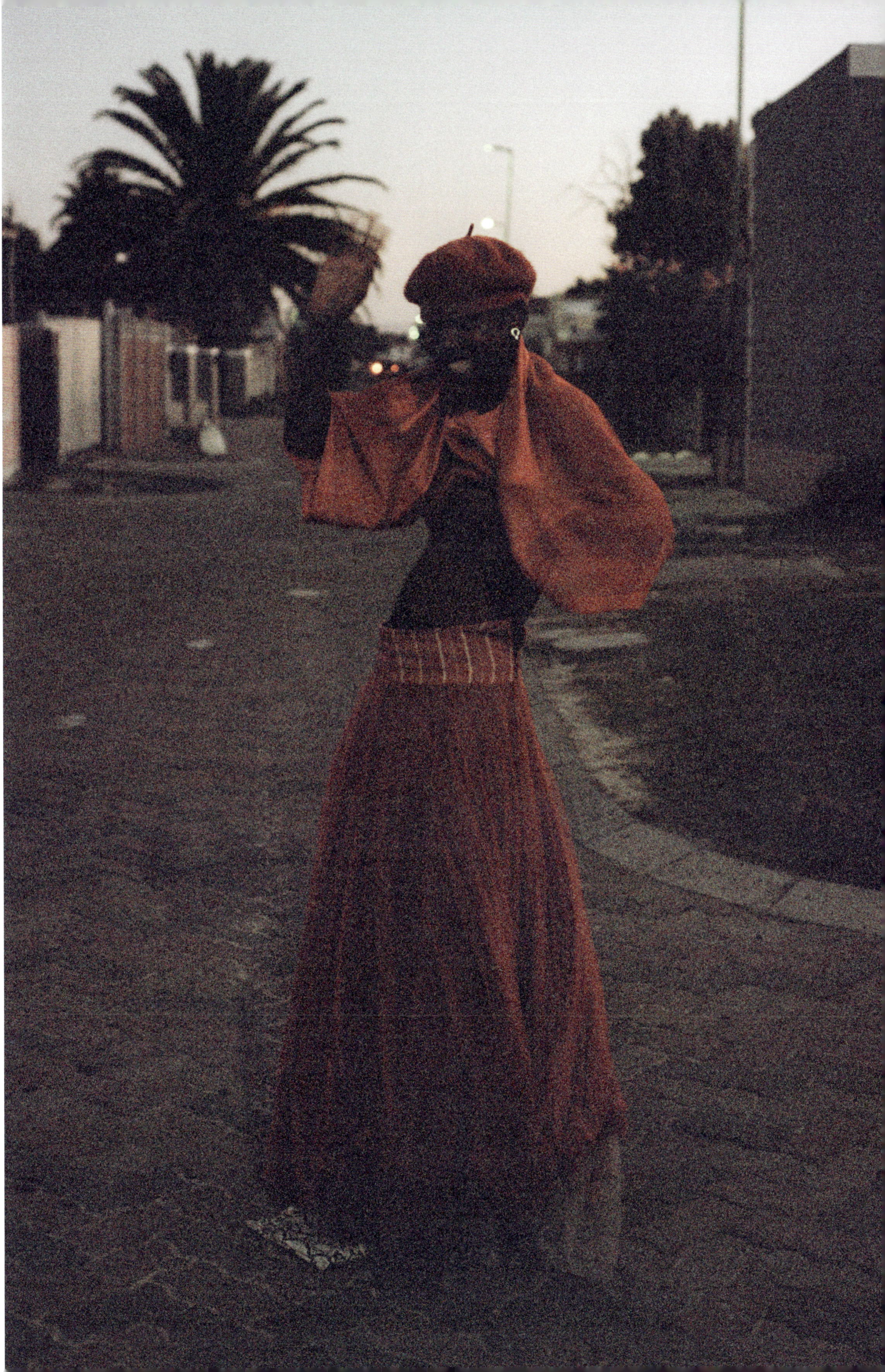

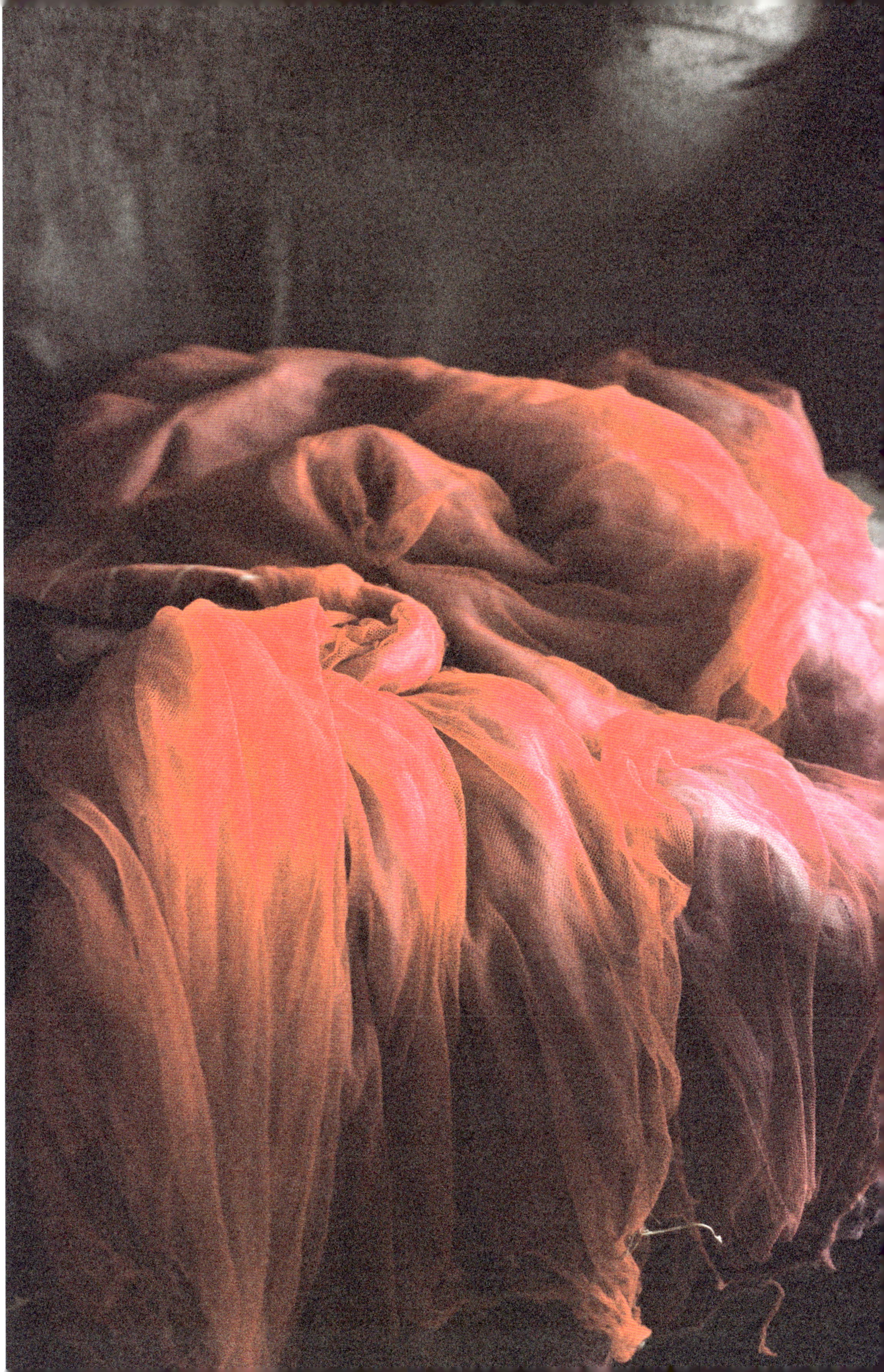

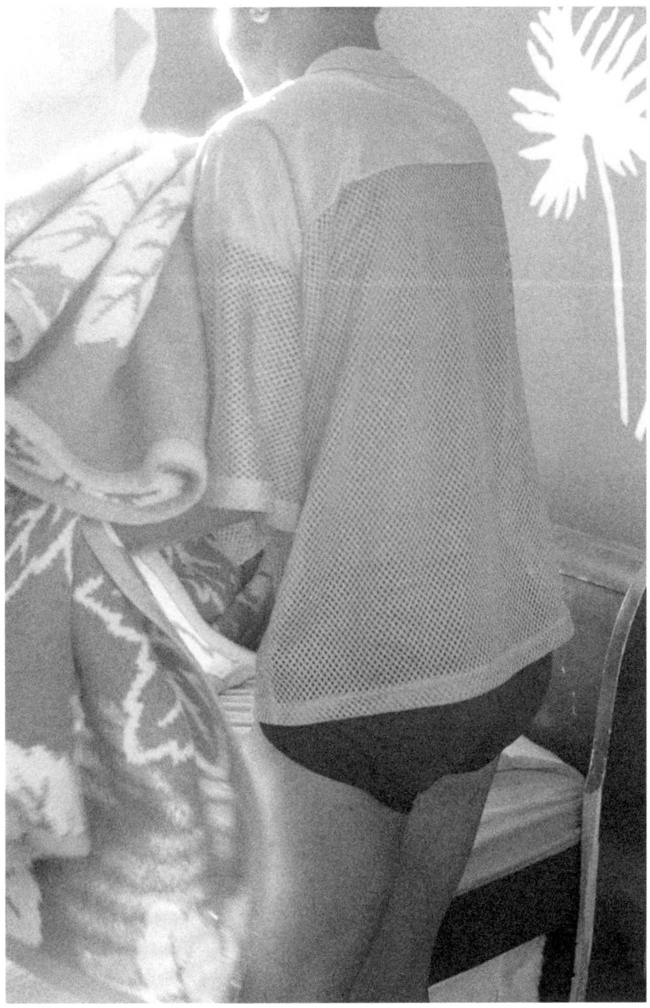

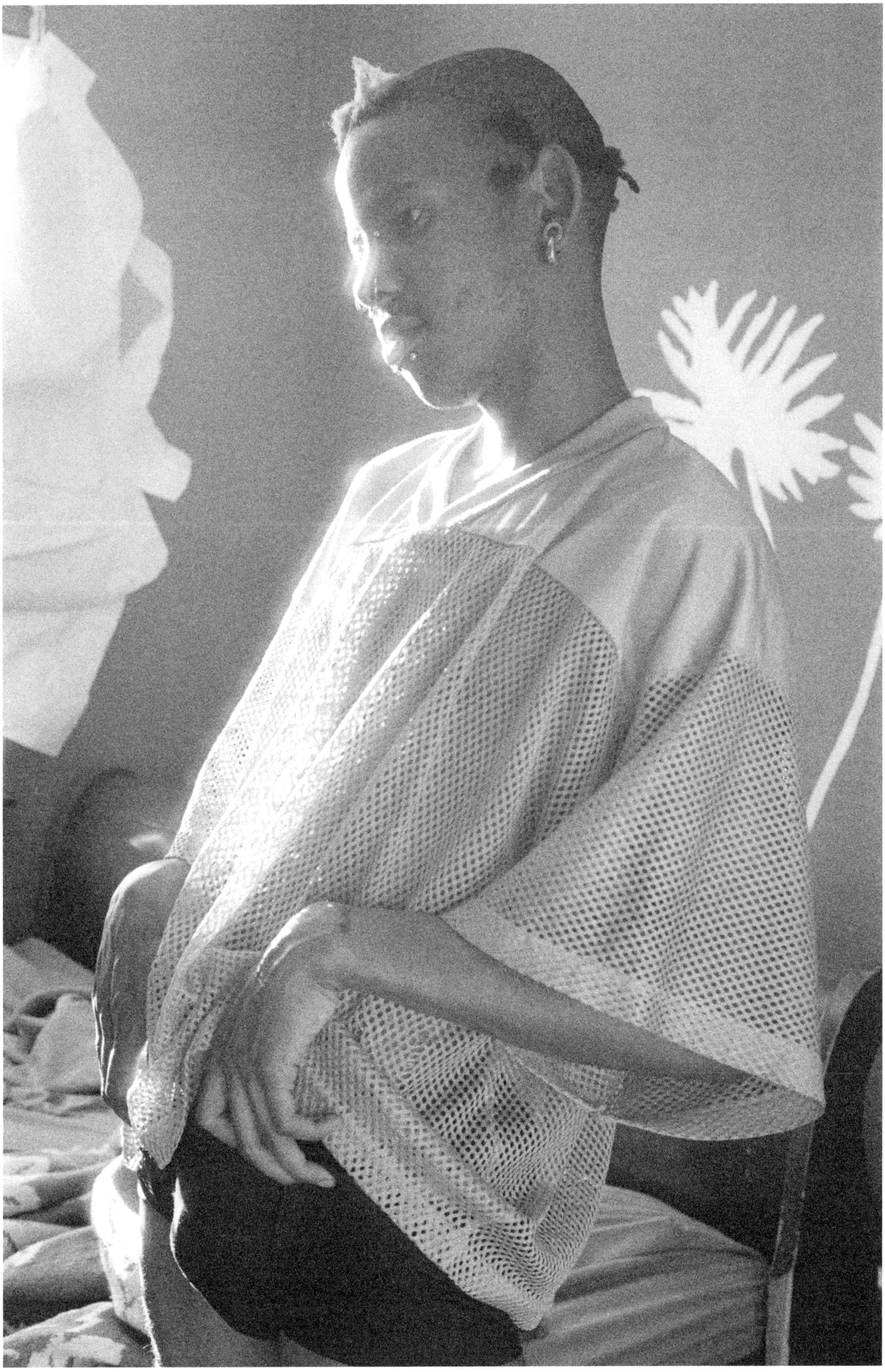

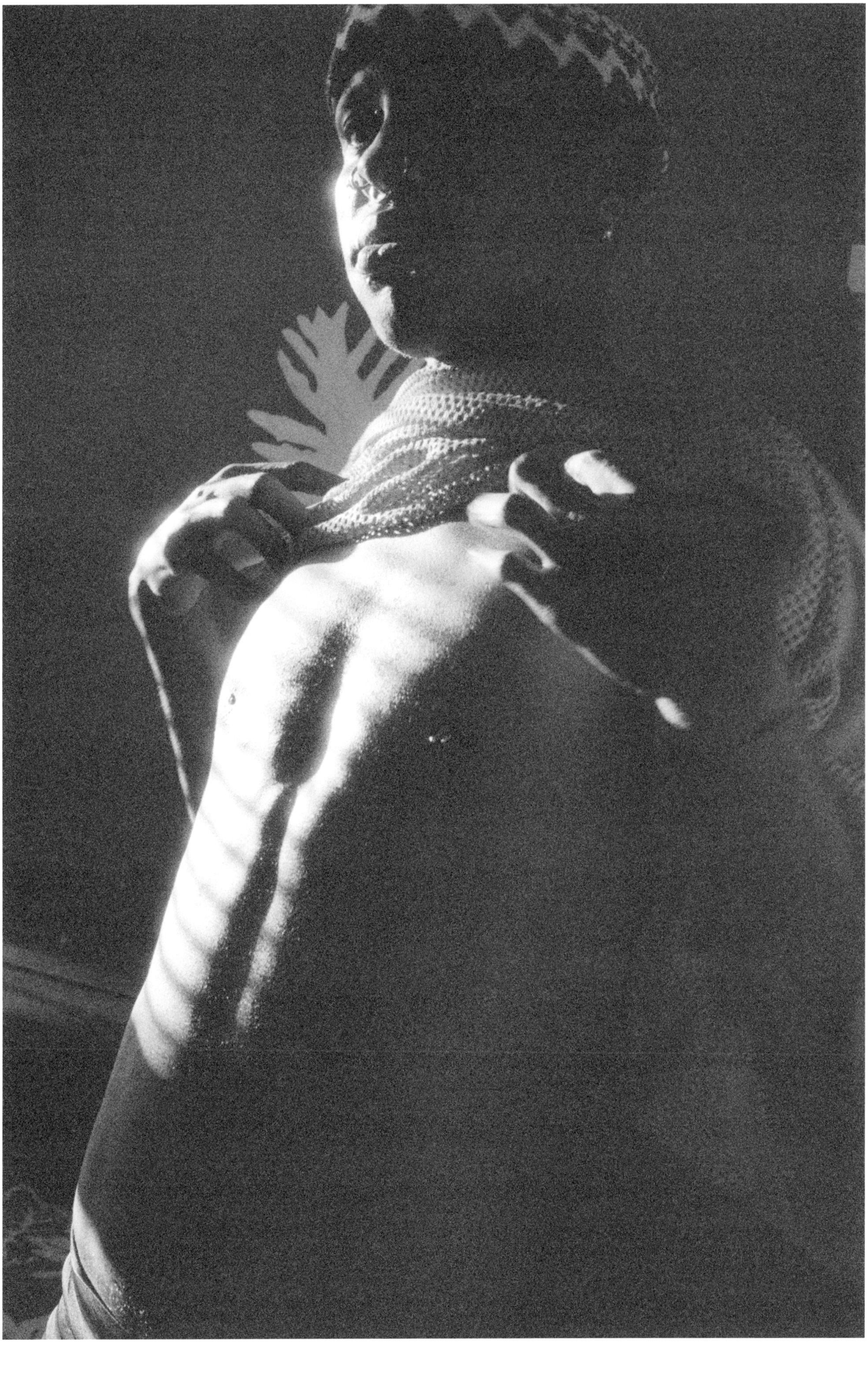

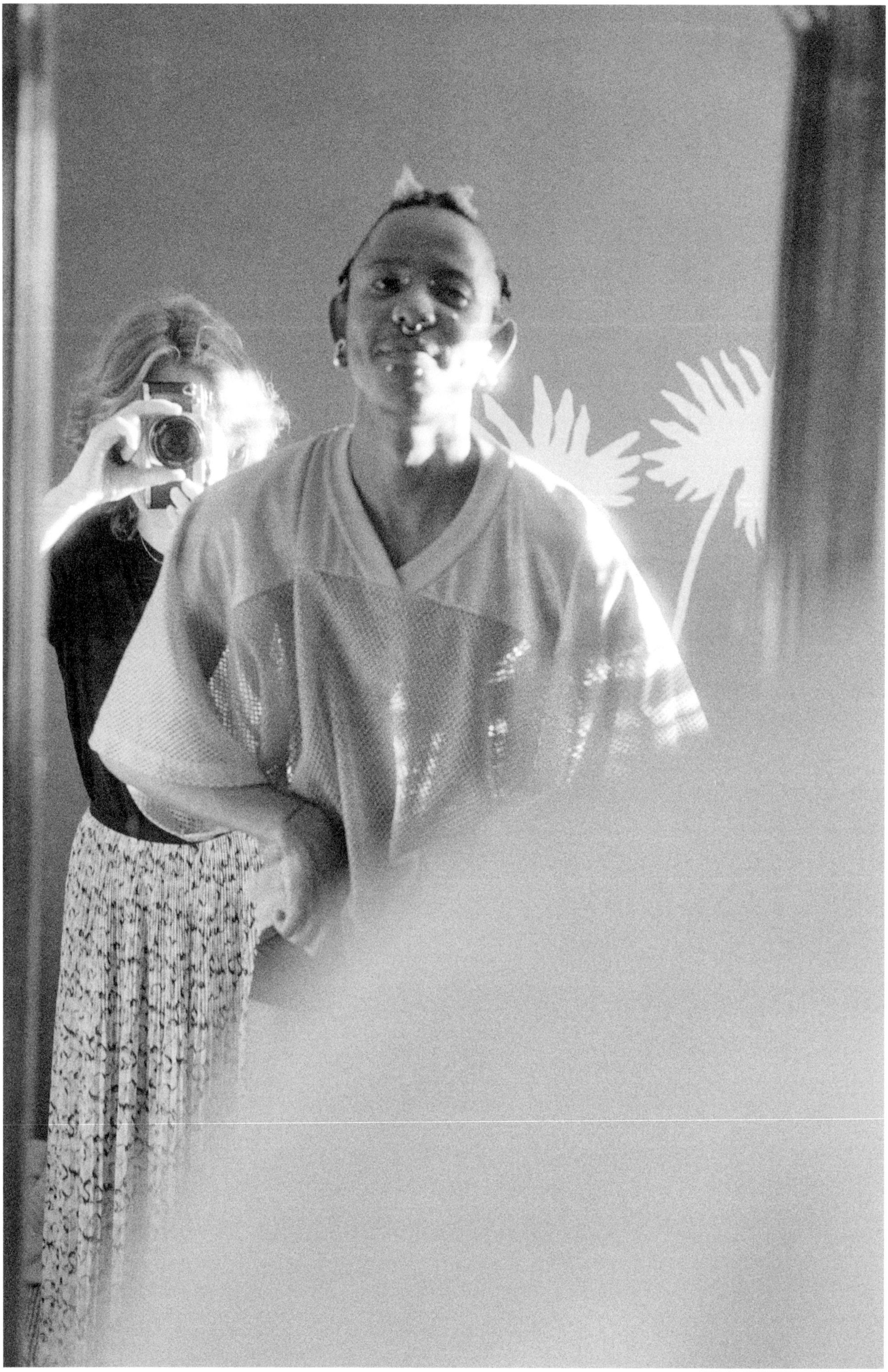

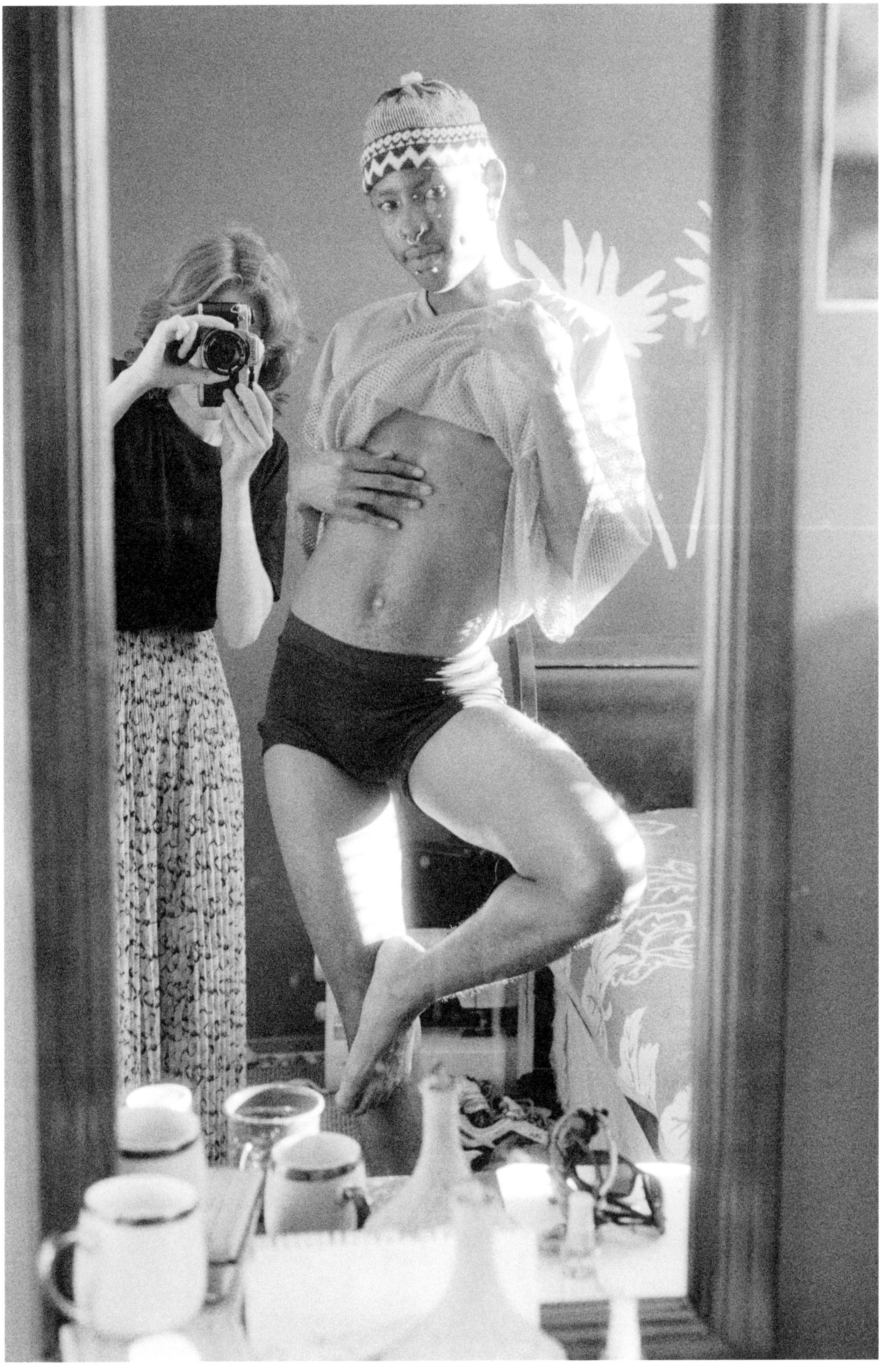

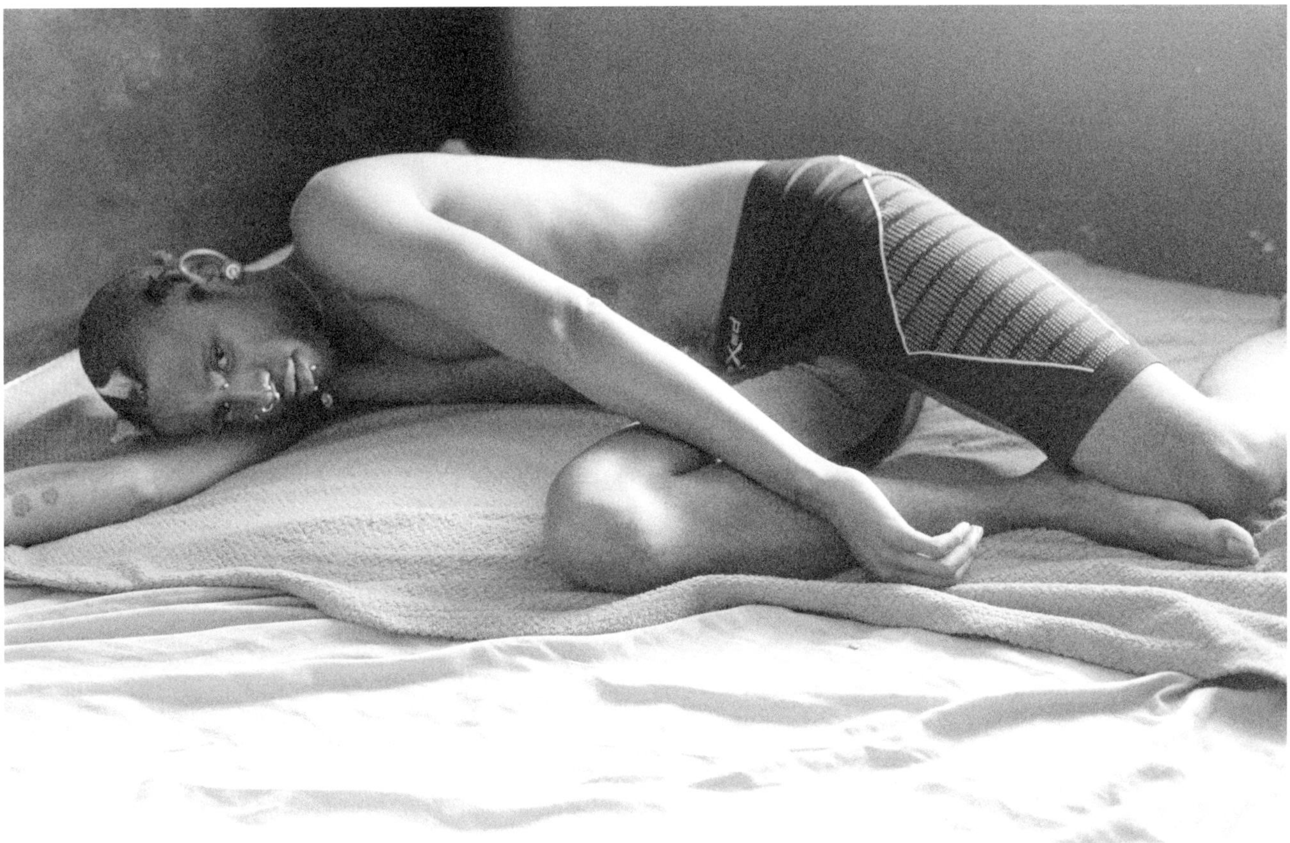

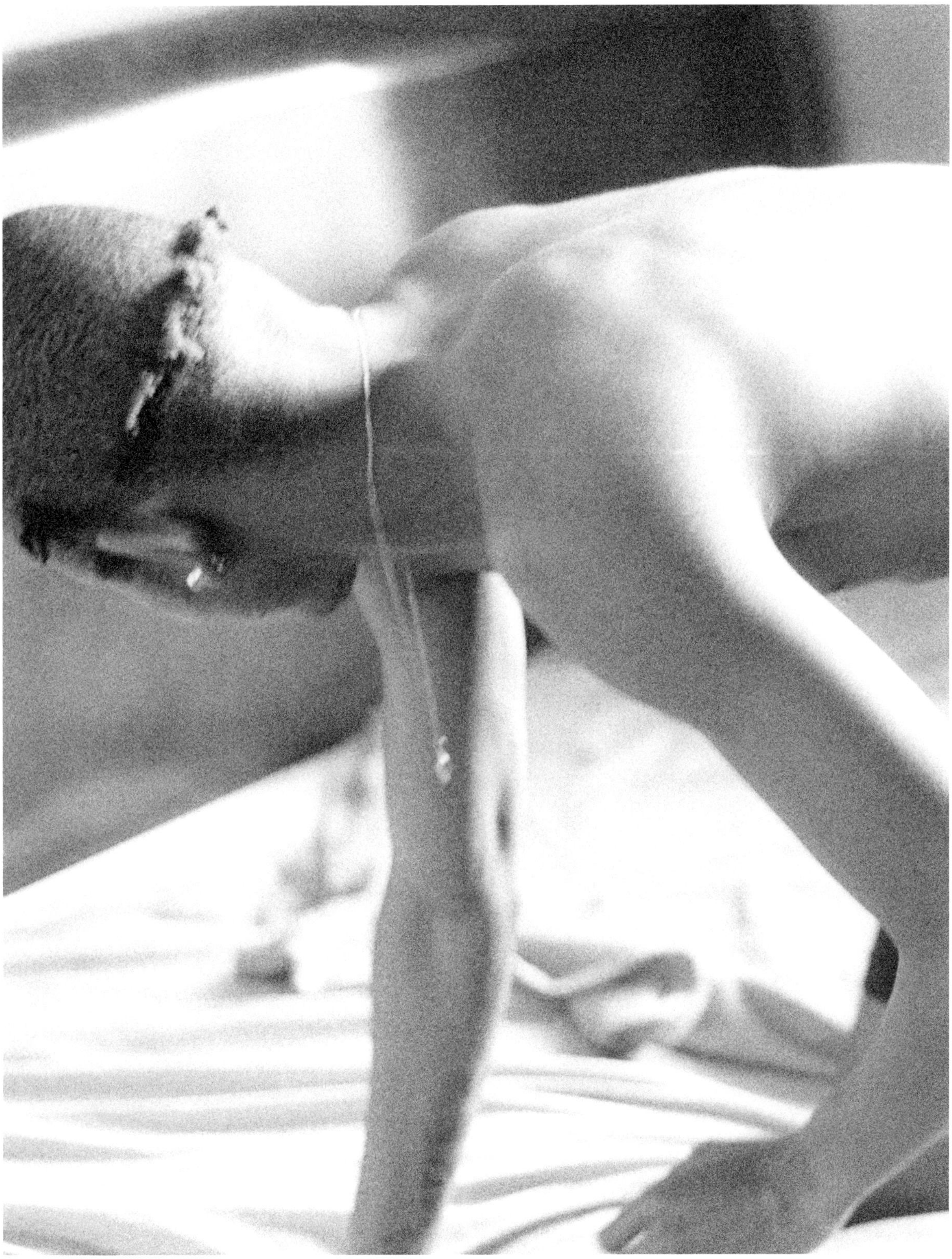

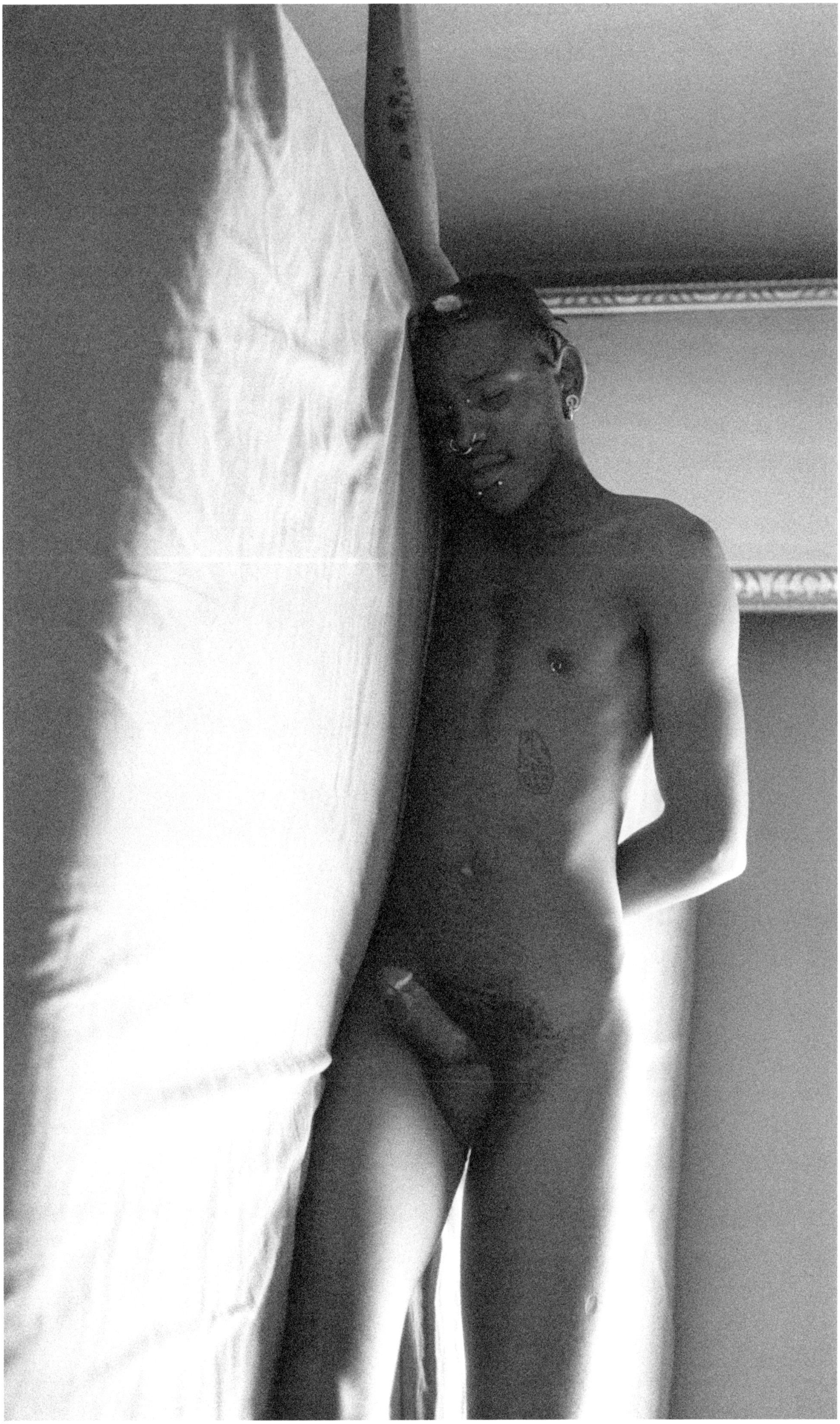

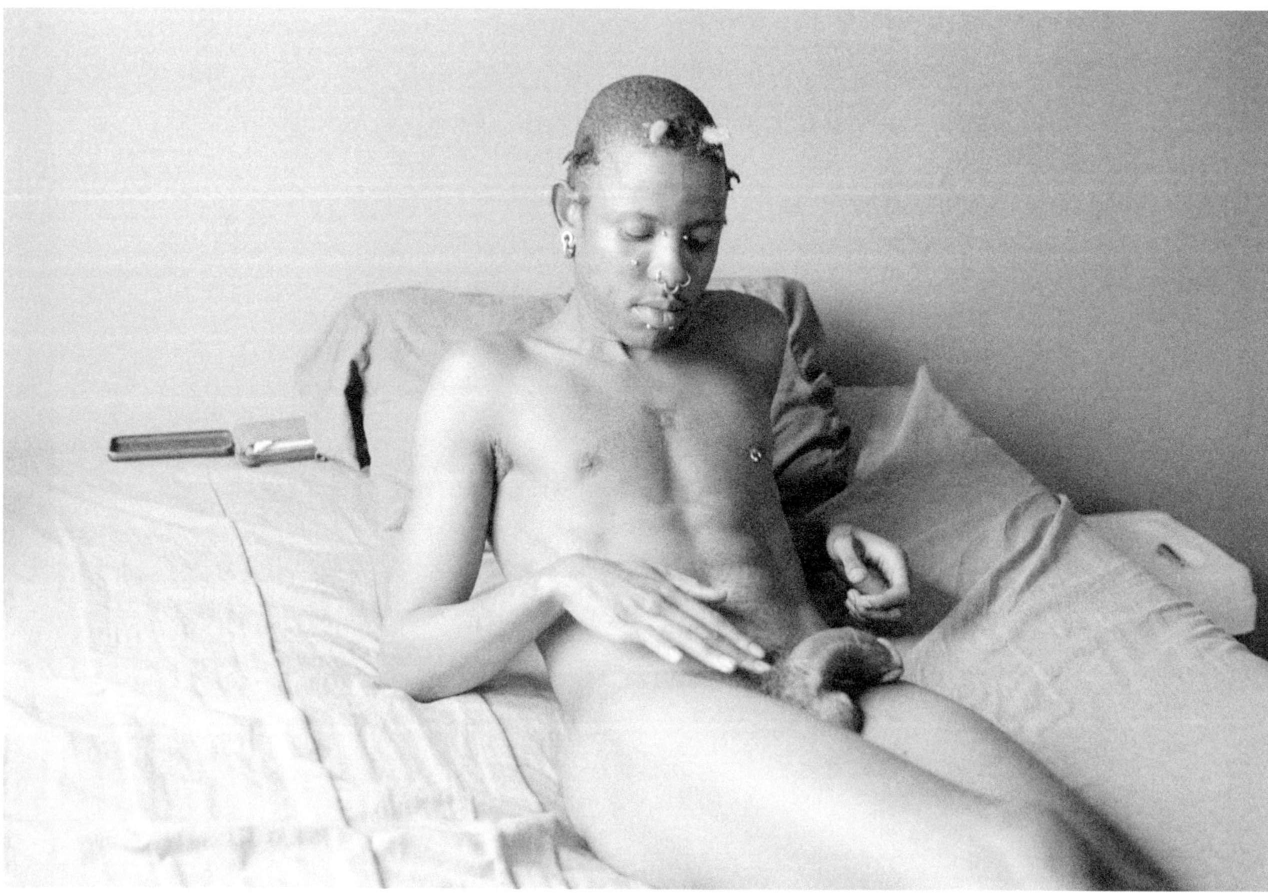

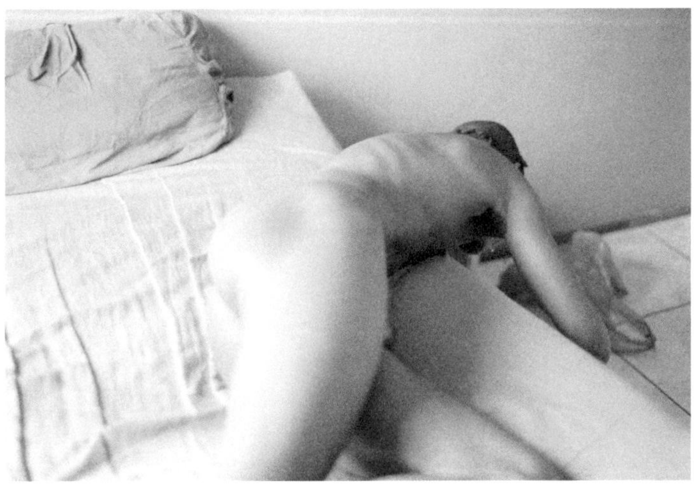

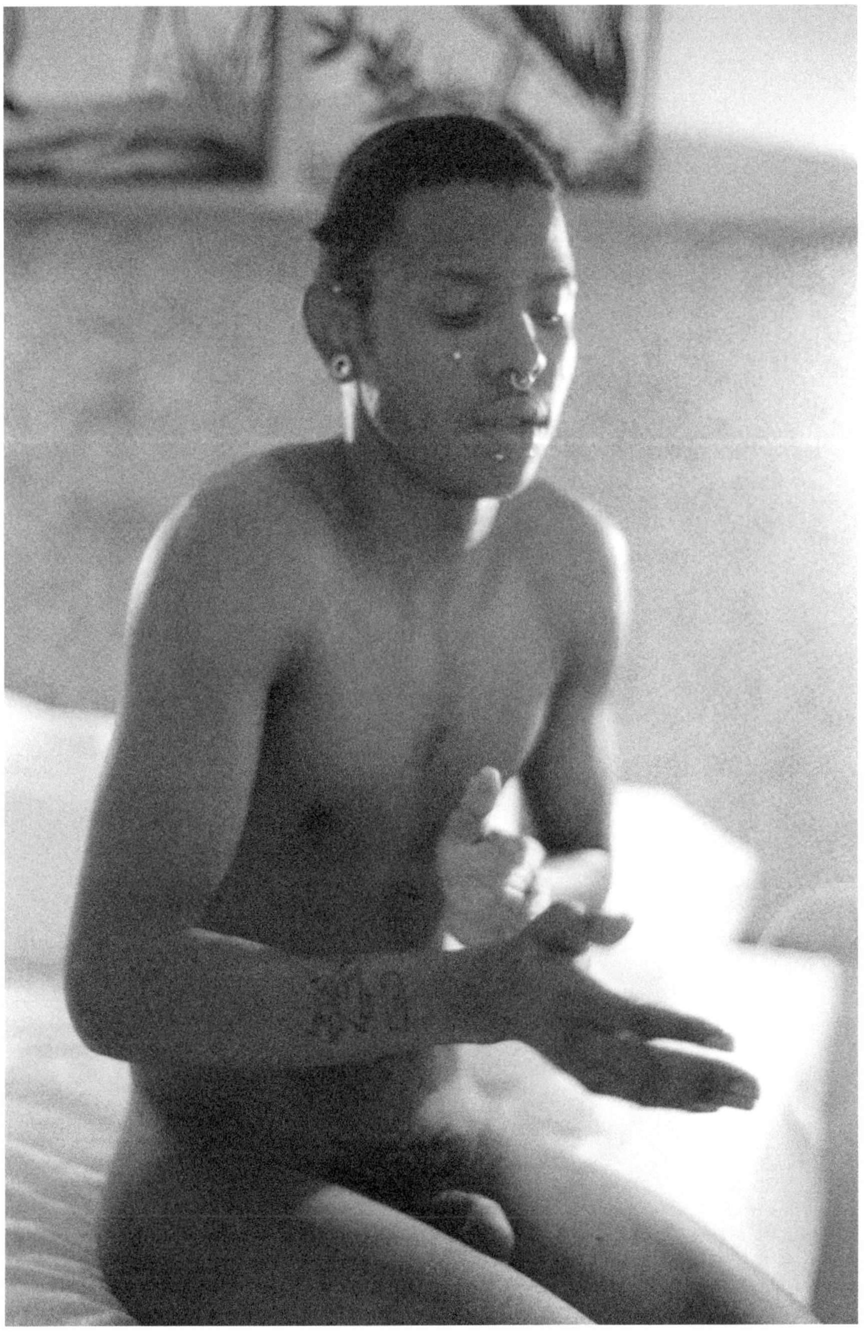

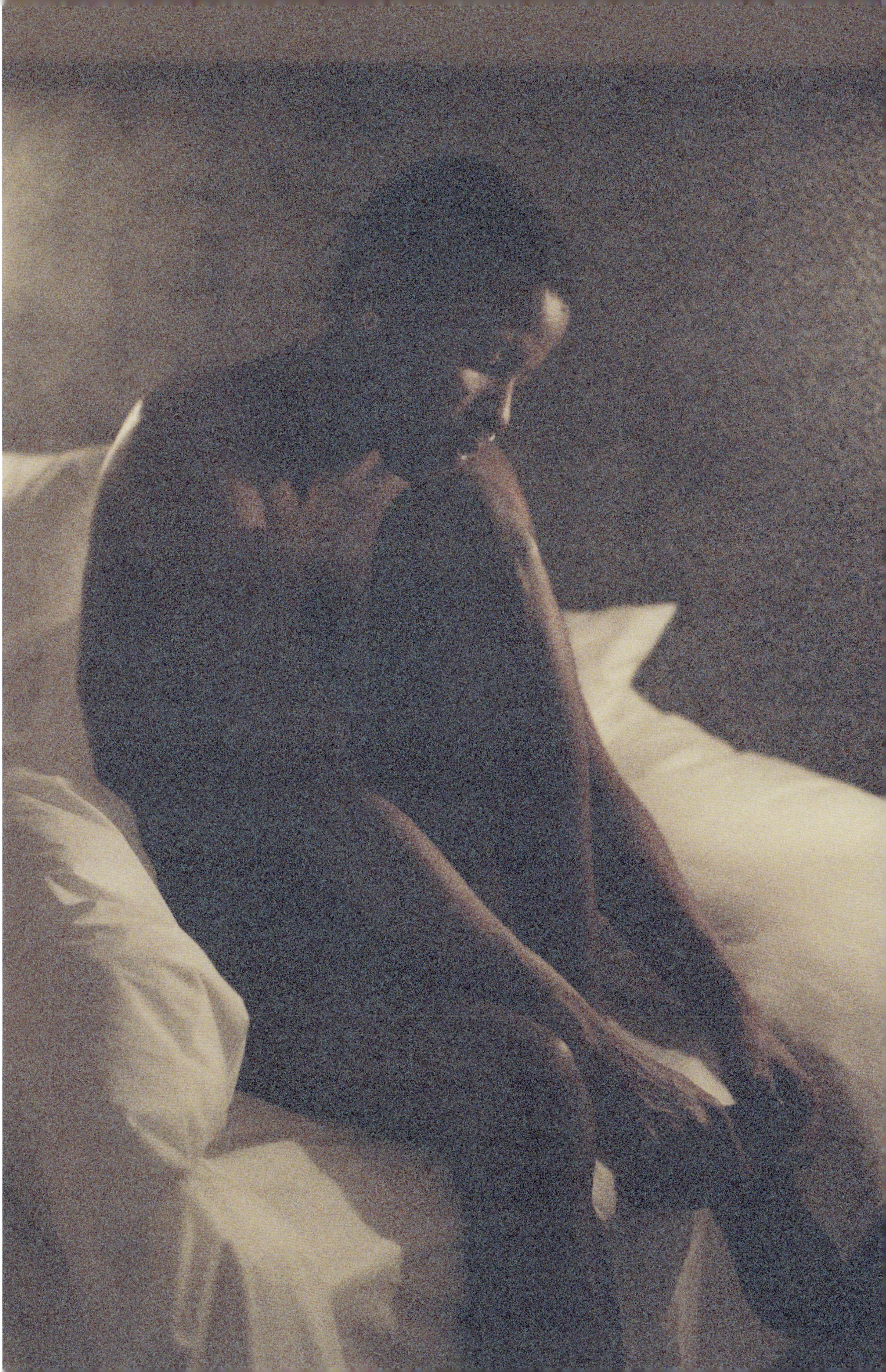

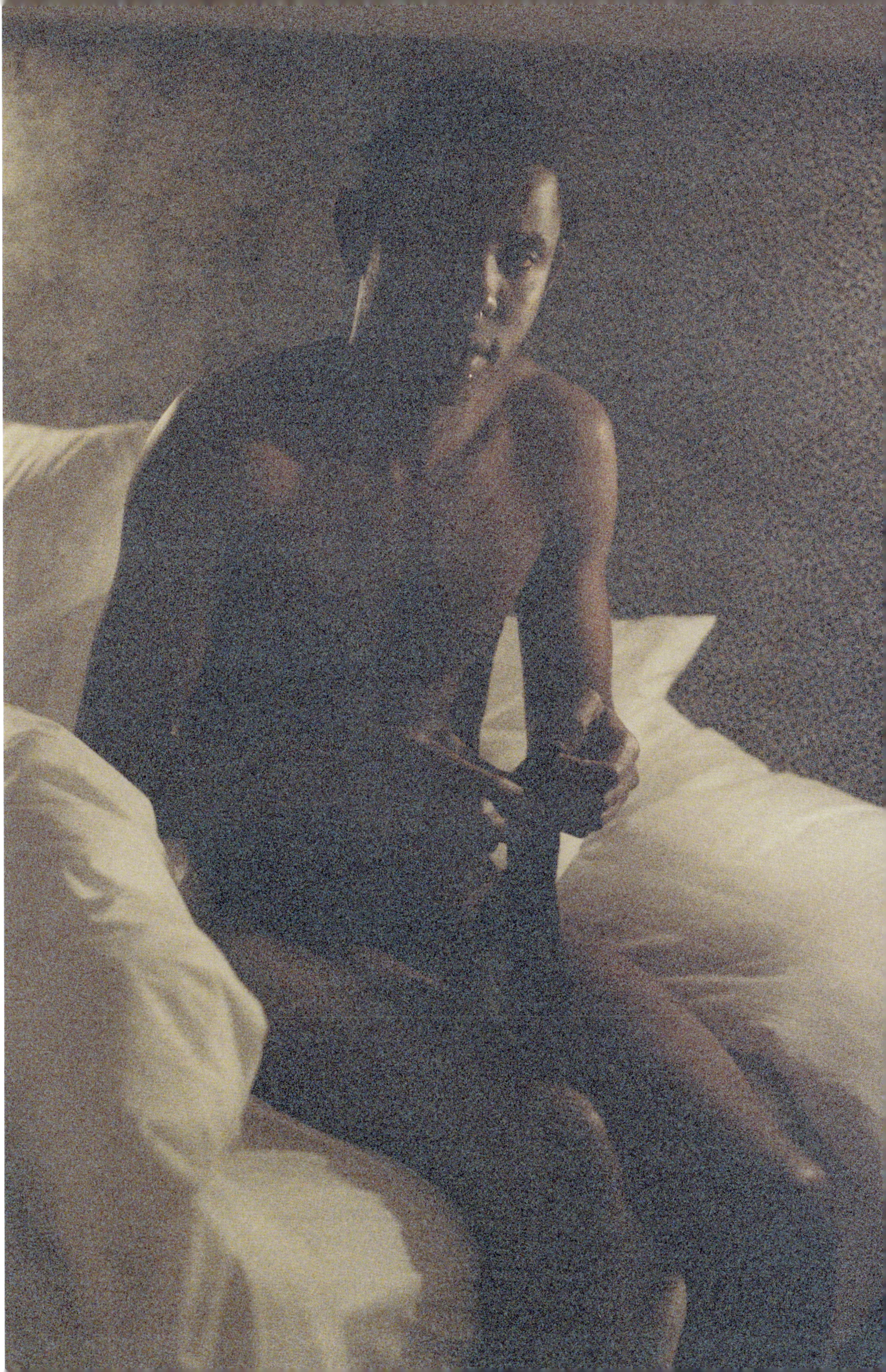

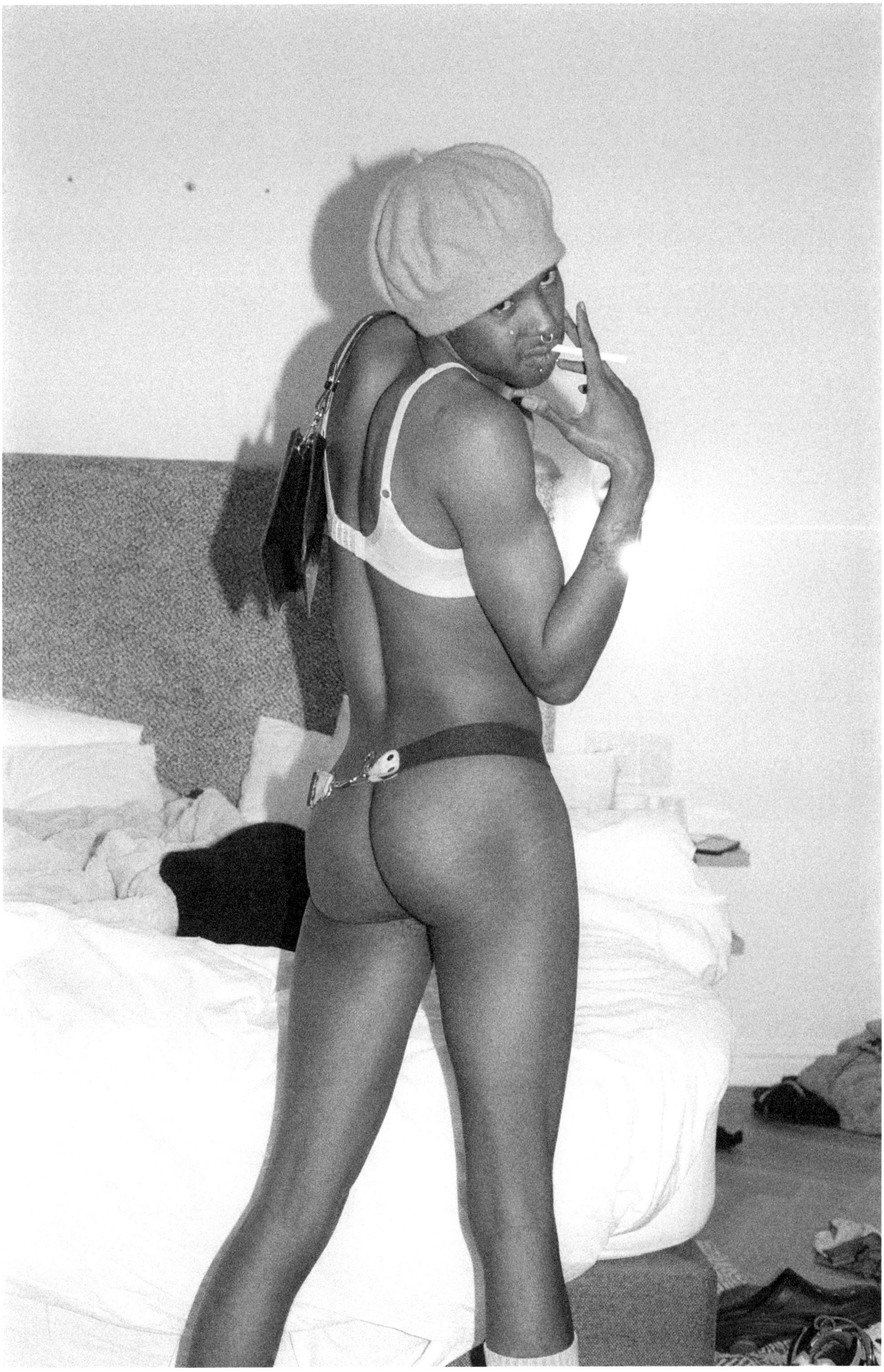

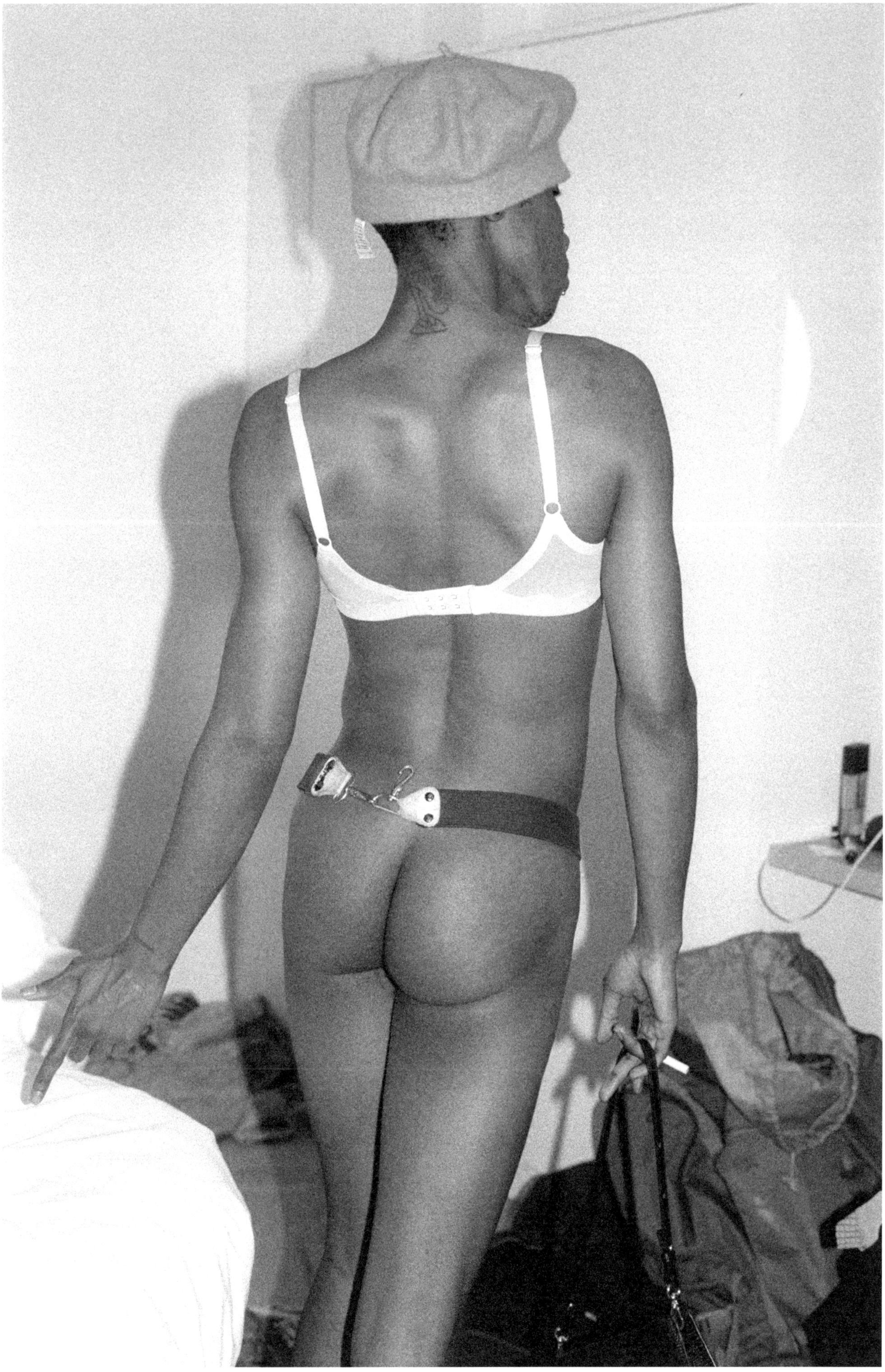

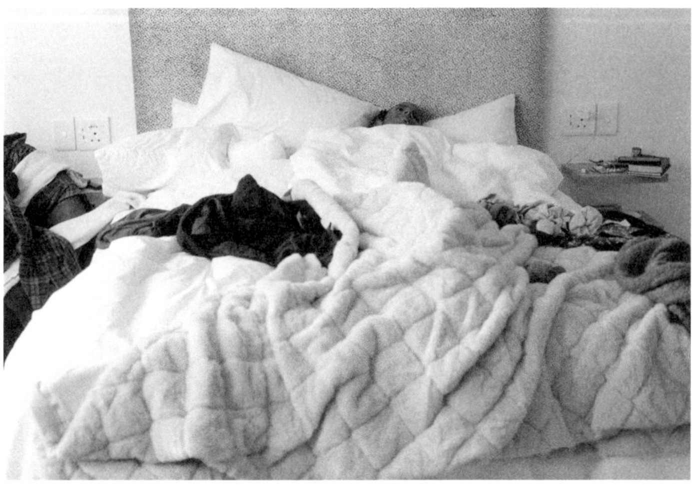

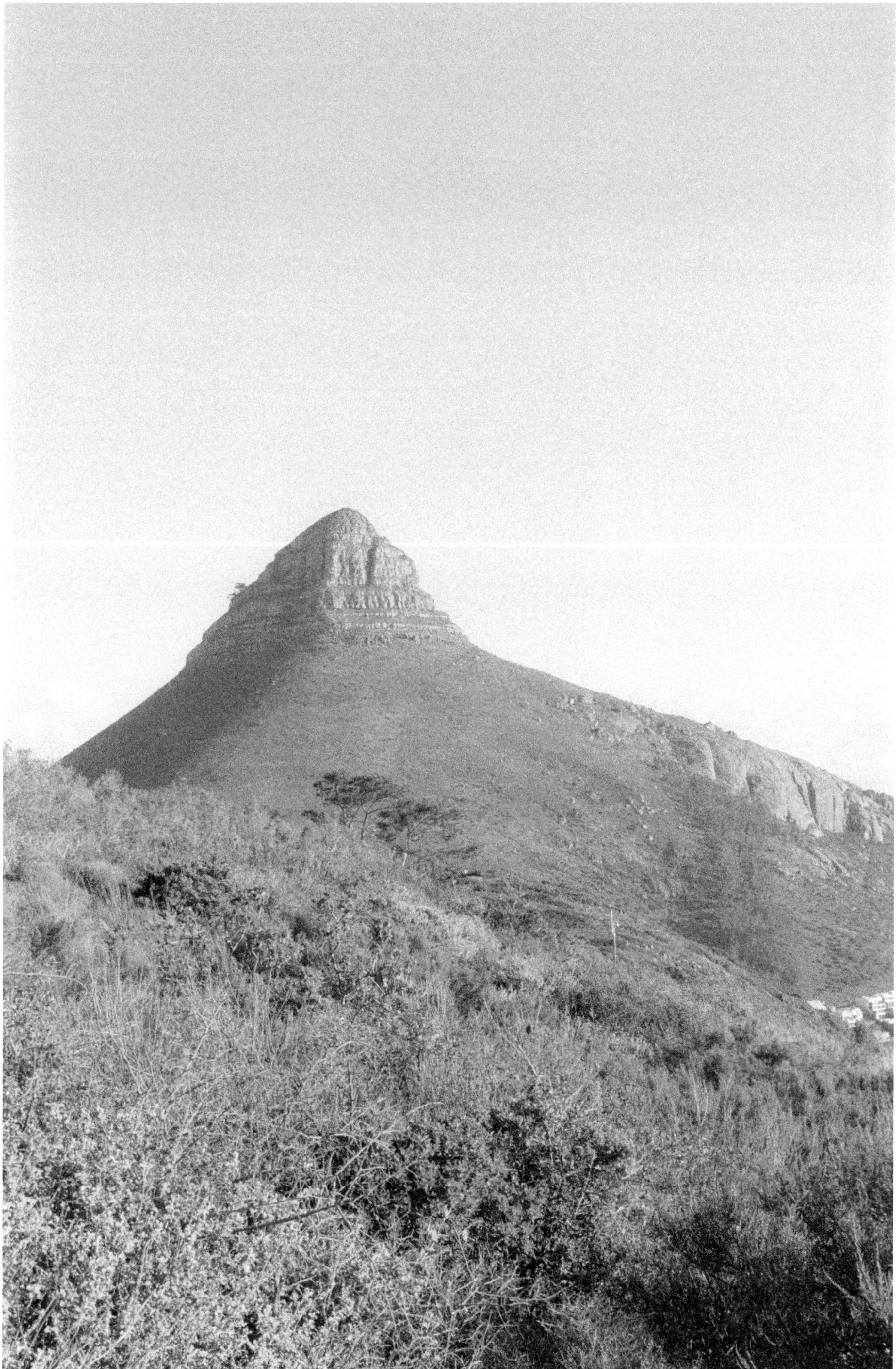

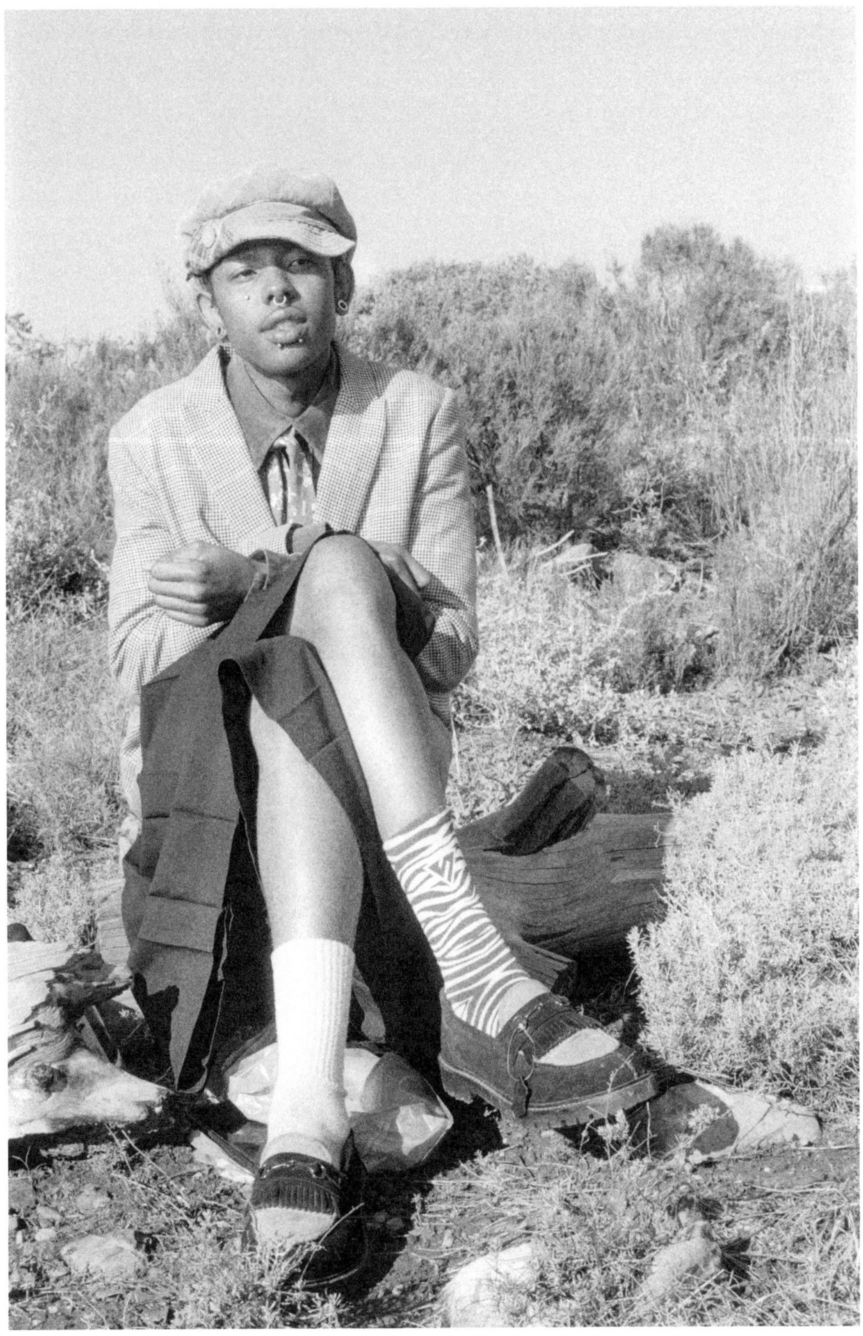

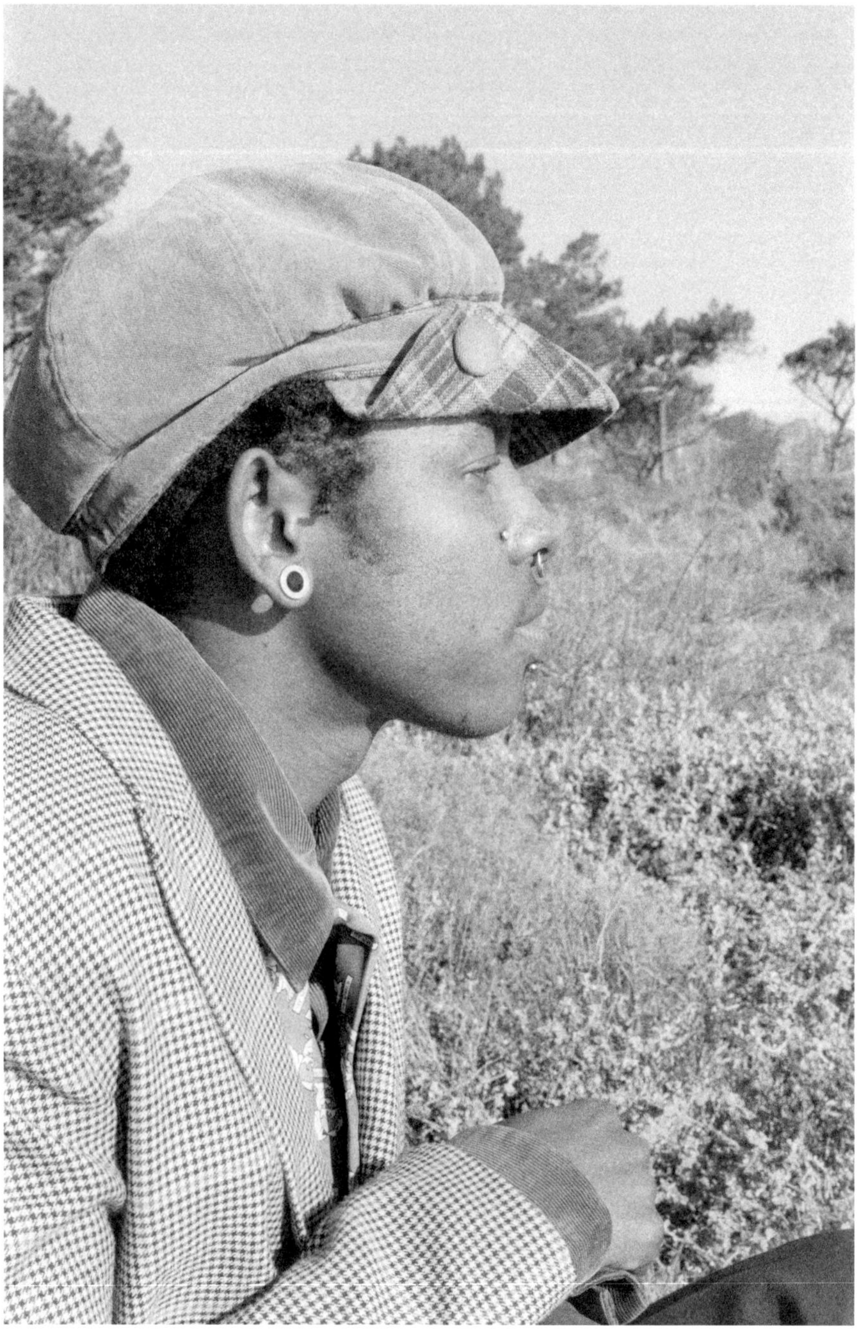

These photographs were made in Summer Greens and on Signal Hill during my two stays in Cape Town between February and July 2024. I first encountered Bathenkosi Sphesihle Luphalule at Broke Klubhouse, where he stood out from the crowd in an orange jumpsuit. Bathenkosi is a stylist and creates clothing occasionally.

Jana Schulz

Sometime in the early stages of 2024, a lady asked if I would be open to a shoot with her. What started as two strangers working for a day slowly became a project between two friends and a camera. We went on to work together for several months, capturing not only the growth in our friendship but also the growth within.

Bathenkosi Sphesihle Luphalule

Editor: Rebecca Wilton
Concept: Jana Schulz
Design: HIT
Text: Logan February
Copy Editing: Stanton Taylor, G&C Art Translators
Image Editing: Carsten Humme, Leipzig
Production Management: Detel Aurand
Printing and Binding: Gutenberg Beuys Feindruckerei, Langenhagen

My heartfelt thanks go to Bathenkosi Sphesihle Luphalule and Neo Timothy, for their collaboration and for allowing me to photograph them. Thanks to Maseng Morake, who always accepted having me around in the house with my camera, and to Natalie Paneng, who introduced me to the city and to Broke Klubhouse.

With the kind support of
Schulze-Fielitz Stiftung Berlin

ISBN 978-3-95476-852-3
Printed in Germany

Published by DISTANZ Verlag
www.distanz.de